THE
ENLIGHTENMENT

THE
ENLIGHTENMENT

A very brief history

ANTHONY KENNY

First published in Great Britain in 2017

Society for Promoting Christian Knowledge
36 Causton Street
London SW1P 4ST
www.spck.org.uk

British Library Cataloguing-in-Publication Data
A catalogue record for this book is available from the British Library

ISBN 978–0–281–07643–7
eBook ISBN 978–0–281–07644–4

Typeset by Manila Typesetting Company
First printed in Great Britain by Ashford Colour Press
Subsequently digitally printed in Great Britain

eBook by Manila Typesetting Company

Produced on paper from sustainable forests

Contents

Part 2
THE LEGACY

Preface

At least a hundred writers contributed to the Enlightenment. If the author of a short book is not to produce a mere roll call of names, he has to make a selection of the most significant thinkers. I have chosen as representatives of the movement Montesquieu, Hume, d'Alembert, Diderot, Lessing, Smith, Franklin, Priestley, Gibbon, Bentham, Paine, Jefferson, Condorcet, Godwin and Wollstonecraft. Other scholars will no doubt disagree with my choice of a first XV, and I must explain that I have included in addition two men who were apostates from the Enlightenment, namely Burke and Rousseau. I have not discussed two German geniuses, Schiller and Goethe, whom I regard as belonging not to the Enlightenment but to the Romantic movement.

Readers may be most surprised that there is no substantial reference to Immanuel Kant. When this short history was first proposed, it was suggested that he should be included within it. I responded that Kant was too great a figure to be treated merely as a member of a movement, and that moreover he, as the father of German idealism, helped to bring the Enlightenment to an end. The publisher's response was to invite me to follow up the present book with one devoted solely to Kant. I look forward to attempting to do justice, so far as the format allows, to his towering genius.

I am indebted to a number of friends and relations who read the text in draft and suggested numerous corrections and improvements: Nancy Kenny, Peter Hacker, Jill Paton Walsh and Charles Kenny. They are of course not responsible for mistakes that remain.

Anthony Kenny

List of abbreviations and conventions

Bentham

B   *The Works of Jeremy Bentham*, ed. John Bowring, 10 vols (New York: Russell & Russell, 1962).

FG   *A Fragment on Government* (London: Wilson & Pickering, 1825).

P   *Introduction to the Principles of Morals and Legislation*, ed. J. H. Burns and H. L. A. Hart (London: Athlone Press, 1982); cited by chapter, section and/or subsection.

Burke

RRF *Reflections on the Revolution in France*, ed. C. C. O'Brien (London: Penguin Classics, 2004).

Diderot

RA   *Le Rêve de d'Alembert*, ed. C. Duflo (Paris: Flammarion, 2002).

Franklin

A   *Autobiography*, ed. O. Seavey (Oxford: Oxford World's Classics, 2008).

Gibbon

DF   *The History of the Decline and Fall of the Roman Empire*, ed. D. Womersley (London: Penguin, 1995).

Hume

E	*An Enquiry Concerning Human Understanding*, ed. Selby Bigge and P. H. Nidditch (Oxford: Clarendon Press, 1928); references are given by page numbers.
ET	*Essays and Treatises* (London: A. Millar, 1768).
HR	*Hume on Religion*, ed. R. Wollheim (London: Collins, 1963).
L	*The Letters of David Hume*, ed. J. Y. T. Greig (Oxford: Clarendon Press, 1969).
T	*A Treatise on Human Nature*, ed. Selby Bigge and P. H. Nidditch (Oxford: Clarendon Press, 1928); references are given by page numbers.

Lessing

GW	*Gesammelte Werke*, ed. K. Lachmann and F. Muncker (Berlin: 1966).

Montesquieu

EL	*De l'esprit des lois*, ed. G. Truc (Paris: Payot, 1945).

Paine

RM	*Rights of Man, Common Sense, and other Political Writings*, ed. M. Philp (Oxford: Oxford World's Classics, 2008).

Rousseau

DI	*Discourse on Inequality*, trans. F. Philip (Oxford: Oxford World's Classics, 2009).
SC	*The Social Contract*, trans. C. Betts (Oxford: Oxford World's Classics, 2008); references are by book and chapter.

Smith

TMS	*The Theory of Moral Sentiments* (Oxford: Oxford University Press, 1976).
WN	*Wealth of Nations*, ed. K. Sutherland (Oxford: Oxford World's Classics, 2008).

Voltaire

C	*Candide and Other Stories*, ed. R. Pearson (Oxford: Oxford World's Classics, 2008).
PD	*Philosophical Dictionary*, ed. T. Besterman (Harmondsworth: Penguin, 1971); cited by page.
TT	*Traité sur la tolérance*, ed. R. Pomeau (Paris: Flammarion, 1989).
BGT	F. Pottle (ed.), *Boswell on the Grand Tour: Germany and Switzerland* (London: Heinemann, 1953).

Chronology

1778   Death of Rousseau
1779   Lessing's *Nathan the Wise*
1779   Hume's *Dialogues*
1780   Lessing's *Education of the Human Race*
1781   Death of Lessing
1789   French Revolution begins with fall of Bastille
1789   Bentham's *Introduction to the Principles of Morals and Legislation*
1790   Death of Franklin
1790   Burke's *Reflections on the Revolution in France*
1791   Paine's *Rights of Man*
1791   Voltaire and Rousseau reburied in Panthéon
1793   Execution of Louis XVI and Marie Antoinette
1794   Death of Gibbon
1797   Death of Burke
1801   Concordat between Napoleon and Pius VII
1804   Napoleon crowns himself Emperor
1815   Battle of Waterloo

Part 1

THE HISTORY

1

The Enlightenment:
when and where?

The Reformation began – so we used to learn at school – when Martin Luther pinned his manifesto on the door of Wittenberg Castle Church on 31 October 1517. The French Revolution began – so we used to learn at school – when the Bastille was stormed on 14 July 1789. No similar day or year is handed down as the starting point of the Enlightenment, and any attempt to assign one is bound to be arbitrary. But if one were forced to choose an initial date, I would suggest 16 April 1746, the date of the Battle of Culloden Moor. It was then and there that the Duke of Cumberland, son of George II, defeated the army of the Young Pretender, Charles Edward Stuart, thus ending his attempt to return the crown of England to the dynasty of his ancestors. It was not that 'Butcher' Cumberland was an enlightened figure: far from it. But Prince Charles' invasion of England, which reached as far as Derby before being turned back, was the last rally in Britain of those institutions that the Enlightenment saw as the forces of darkness. For Charles was a member of the Roman Catholic Church, and in politics a proponent of absolute rule, being himself the great grandson of the monarch who had proclaimed the divine right of kings.

While in Britain Culloden marked the end of the pre-enlightenment era, France was still ruled by an absolute monarch, and French life was in many ways controlled by a Catholic hierarchy. None the less, the same decade marks the launch of the Enlightenment there. In recent decades there has been considerable debate about where to locate the centre of the Enlightenment. Was the movement fundamentally a French phenomenon, as people long believed? Or did it originate in Britain and reach its consummation in Germany, as different scholars have argued? The entire argument, in my view, obscures the point that the Enlightenment was essentially an international phenomenon, and that was how it was seen by its participants.

Leaders of the French Enlightenment, such as Montesquieu and Voltaire, spent formative years in England; of their British counterparts, Hume wrote his first work in Anjou, Gibbon for half of his life thought in French, and Priestley and Bentham were among the first citizens of the French Republic. While Voltaire wanted France to become more like England, Hume thought that life in Paris was infinitely preferable to life in London. Voltaire and Diderot accepted invitations to spread the word in Berlin and in St Petersburg. Finally, one of the finest embodiments of the Enlightenment's scientific and political ideals was an American, Benjamin Franklin, who spent large parts of his life in London and Paris.

In the year 1746 most of the principal figures of the movement were alive and active, but their major contributions to the Enlightenment lay in the future. Montesquieu was 57, but he was yet to publish *De l'esprit des lois*. Voltaire was 52, but it would be 18 years yet before he published his *Philosophical Dictionary*. Hume was by now 32, and had at an early age published his *A Treatise on Human Nature*, but it fell, in his own words, 'deadborn from the Press'. It was Hume's later work, some of it published only posthumously, that made a decisive contribution to the Enlightenment. Of the editors of the future *Encyclopédie*, Diderot was 33 and d'Alembert was 29. Adam Smith was only 23, and his *Wealth of Nations* lay 30 years in the future. The two founding fathers of the enlightenment discipline of aesthetics, Lessing and Burke, were both just 17. Two of the youngest enlightenment heroes were still children: Tom Paine and Edward Gibbon were both nine years old. Two men who in different ways would bring the enlightenment project to its conclusion – Jean-Jacques Rousseau and Immanuel Kant – were in their early twenties.

The enlightenment philosophers – and *philosophes* was what in France they most liked to call themselves – held many things in common. They rejected the great continental metaphysical systems of the previous century, such as those of Descartes and Leibniz (some made an exception for Spinoza). Instead they admired the physics of Newton and the epistemology of Locke. One of Voltaire's earliest works was entitled *Éléments de la philosophie de Newton*, and he and his colleagues rejected Descartes' theory of innate ideas. They all believed that the way to discover truth about the world is the systematic use of the senses – such as sight and hearing – in investigation and exploration. They believed that scientific endeavour depended on observation and experiment, and that its progress would lead to the betterment of the human condition.

In this they were following the lead of Locke, but Locke himself believed that experience provided not only the method of science but the object of science. He insisted that the only kind of certainty we can achieve is not really about the world in itself but only the deliveries of our senses and imagination, the items he called 'ideas'. Ideas and thoughts are what we meet when we look within ourselves. Some of his followers went further and claimed that ideas, and the sensory impressions from which they derive, are all that we can ever really know. This extreme form of empiricism is a philosophical blind alley, as later philosophers were to show, notably the greatest philosopher at the end of the enlightenment period, Immanuel Kant.

However, not all the *philosophes* were extreme empiricists, and the form of empiricism that each of them adopted affected the way they set out to follow the lead of Newton. Franklin, using the experimental method, made genuine scientific discoveries about the real world. Hume, an extreme empiricist, set out to do for psychology what Newton had done for physics: he aimed to provide an account of the relationships of ideas that would be a counterpart to the gravitational attraction between bodies. But because he based himself on introspection rather than observation and experiment, he produced a philosophy of mind that turned out to be ultimately futile. Fortunately, his contributions to enlightenment thinking were not vitiated by the flaws in his theoretical philosophy.

In matters of politics, enlightenment thinkers shared a common antipathy to arbitrary rule and its various manifestations: judicial torture, imprisonment without trial, proliferation of capital punishments and corruption of tribunals. However, the path to reform they proposed differed from one country to another depending on the nature of the status quo. Where there was an absolute monarch, his or her power should be subjected to some external restraint, if only by allowing their subjects freedom of speech. In a constitutional monarchy, and even in a republic, there must be a separation of powers between executive, legislature and judiciary. As Gibbon was to put it, 'the principles of a free constitution are irrecoverably lost, when the legislative power is nominated by the executive' (*DF* I. 66). Democracy, however, was not initially a key goal of the Enlightenment. Voltaire and Diderot were content to work for despots, and the last thing they aimed at was the empowerment of what Voltaire called 'the rabble'. They protested against the abuse of power by governments but did not propose fundamental political change. That came to the fore only in the later stages of the Enlightenment, in particular in the writings of Tom Paine. However, along the political axis that has autocracy at one end and anarchy at the other, the enlightenment figures, wherever they were placed, shared a common direction of movement away from autocracy.

In matters of religion it was a common feature of the Enlightenment to value reason above faith. Few enlightenment thinkers were outright atheists, but on the continent they were fiercely anti-clerical, and in Britain they were at least sceptical about the supernatural. Individuals' views of Christianity were aligned along a spectrum from suspicion to hostility. Few were any longer prepared to accept the Bible as an unerring guide to the truth. Many were deists; that is, they believed that reason could establish the existence of a creator God but not of a God who intervened in human history or offered a revelation through sacred texts. The variety of religious sects, according to the Enlightenment, provided a reason for toleration rather than enforced conformity. As the century progressed, many moved further and further from the orthodoxy of the established churches. Some saw it as a moment of triumph for the Enlightenment when a goddess of reason was enthroned in the Cathedral of Notre Dame by French revolutionaries in 1793.

The Enlightenment was a network rather than a school: there were few settled doctrines that were common to all the *philosophes*. It was a movement rather than a party: its members shared a common direction rather than a common platform. Immanuel Kant, writing in 1784, asked himself whether he was living in an enlightened age. No, he replied: only in an age of gradual enlightening, an age approaching enlightenment.

2

President Montesquieu

The first major attempt to present an enlightened under-standing of the human social and political condition was the work of Charles-Louis de Secondat, Baron de Montesquieu (1689–1755). His *The Spirit of the Laws* was published in 1748 and drew on a mass of historical and sociological eru-dition to build up a theory of the nature of the state. The volume took many years to compose, and it was preceded by a lighter working-up of some of its material in the form of an epistolary novel, the *Persian Letters* of 1721.

The novel relates the travels in Europe of two Persians, the patriarch Usbek and his youthful companion Rica. Their letters home express their surprise and astonishment at many features of Christian culture that Europeans take for granted. They report, for instance, that in Paris, in reverse of the Persian custom, the men wear trousers and the women wear skirts. The narrative offers a vehicle for sat-ire on French society and on institutions like the papacy and the Inquisition. However, in the course of their jour-neys the travellers become aware of the weaknesses as well as the strengths of the Islamic society they have left at home. For Montesquieu, universal and fundamental human needs and passions find a variety of expressions in radically diverse cultures. He illustrates this with reference, among other things, to various possible arrangements for relationships between the sexes. He goes so far as to imagine

9

a female paradise in which the women will possess their own seraglio where the men are confined under the guard of eunuchs.

The Spirit of the Laws is a more ponderous presentation of a similar theme. In accordance with enlightenment methodology it assembles a massive, if not wholly reliable, database of geographical, historical and anthropological material. 'Men', Montesquieu tells us, 'are governed by many factors: climate, religion, law, the precepts of government, the examples of the past, customs, manners; and from the combination of such influences there arises a general spirit' (*EL* 6.6). The general spirit of a particular society finds its expression in the laws appropriate for it: it creates 'the spirit of the laws', which gives the treatise its title.

Montesquieu believed that there were fundamental laws of justice established by God, which held in advance of any human legislation. But these universal principles did not themselves suffice to determine the structure of any particular society. No single set of social institutions was suitable for all times and places: the government should be fitted to the climate, the wealth and the national character of a country. Humans are always and everywhere subject to the same passions, which fall within the scope of a supreme natural law; but this law has to be expressed in different systems in accordance with the external conditions of each society.

Following the lead of Aristotle, Montesquieu classified the constitutions he had collected into three types: republican, monarchical, and despotic (*EL* 2.1). In a despotic state, government is by the decree of the ruler, backed up not by law but by religion or custom. In a monarchy, government is carried on by a hierarchy of officials of varied rank and status. In a republic, all the citizens need to be educated in civic values and trained to carry out public tasks.

The dominant characteristic of a republican state is virtue; the other two states are dominated respectively by honour and fear. Montesquieu does not mean that in a given republic people are virtuous, but that they ought to be. Again he does not mean that in each monarchy people have a sense of honour, and that in each despotic state everyone is ruled by fear. However, unless these features predominate, the relevant type of government will fail to function smoothly (*EL* 3.2).

'Liberty', we are told, 'has its roots in the soil.' Freedom is easier to defend in mountainous or insular countries than in ample and fertile plains. Consequently a republican constitution suits cold climates and small states, while despotism suits large states and hot climates. A constitution suitable for Sicilians would not suit Scotsmen since, inter alia, sea-girt islands differ from mountainous mainlands. Among the various possible constitutions, Montesquieu's own preference is for monarchy, and particularly the 'mixed monarchy' he discerned in England.

The feature Montesquieu admired in the British constitution was the principle of the separation of powers. After the revolution of 1688, Parliament had achieved sole legislative power, while leaving in practice considerable executive discretion to the King's ministers. Simultaneously, judges became largely free of governmental interference. To be sure, there was not to be found in British constitutional law any explicit statement that the legislative, executive and judicial branches of government should not be combined in a single person or institution. The present-day UK Supreme Court is a very young institution, only recently detached from the House of Lords, which is a branch of the legislature. In Britain there has never been a constitutionally formulated theory of checks and balances. None the less, Montesquieu's benign interpretation of the contemporary British system, in which the sovereign's ministers essentially depended for their power on the consent of Parliament, was to have a lasting influence on constitution makers in many parts of the world. In particular it became entrenched in the constitution of the United States, where its effects are, for better or worse, perceptible to this day.

The separation of powers was important, Montesquieu believed, because it provided the best bulwark against tyranny and the best guarantee of the liberty of the subject. What, then, is liberty? 'Liberty', Montesquieu replies, 'is a right of doing whatever the laws permit' (*EL* 11.3). Is that all, we may wonder: doesn't even a citizen of a tyranny enjoy that much freedom? We must first remember that for Montesquieu, a despot ruled not by law but by decree: for him only an instrument created by an independent legislature counts as a law. Second, in many countries, including the France of Montesquieu's own time, citizens were often at risk of arbitrary arrest for actions that were perfectly legal but regarded as offensive by those in power. But political liberty, Montesquieu believed, could never be absolute. Free trade did not mean that traders could do whatever they liked: they must be constrained by laws that protected the common interest.

Montesquieu also offered another, more substantial, definition of liberty. It consists not in freedom from all restraint but 'in the power of doing what we ought to will and in not being constrained to do what we ought not to will' (*EL* 11.3). This link between liberal social institutions and an idealized form of the individual will was later to be developed into a substantial political theory by Jean-Jacques Rousseau in his *Social Contract.*

Montesquieu believed in the existence of a benevolent God, who was the author of the natural law and had given human beings freedom to follow or to break that law. Atheism he found repellent: the idea of a godless universe was terrifying. However, for much of his life Montesquieu sat very loose to Catholic doctrine, and *The Spirit of the Laws,* when it appeared, was placed on the Index of forbidden books by Pope Benedict XIV. In accordance with his general sociological principles about the relationship between social institutions and the physical environment, Montesquieu seems to have believed that in France, Catholicism was the appropriate religion, while Protestantism was appropriate for England. But for all places he was a keen advocate of toleration, and though he was reconciled to the Church on his deathbed, he always allowed his wife to retain the Protestantism in which she had been brought up.

3

Hume on miracles

In the same year that the *Spirit of the Laws* appeared, David Hume published his first contribution to the philosophy of religion, an essay on miracles. The essay had been written years earlier when he was writing the *Treatise on Human Nature* but it was not included in the published version of that work. By 1748 Hume was less afraid of giving offence, and the text appeared as Section 10 of the *Philosophical Essays concerning Human Understanding* (later known as *An Enquiry concerning Human Understanding*). It immediately caused a sensation, since it undercut the use of miracles by apologists to claim supernatural authorization for a particular religious message.

Hume begins the essay by distinguishing between proof and probability: a wise person proportions his or her belief to the evidence. If the evidence for a particular conclusion is incontrovertible, we accept the conclusion as proved. If there is evidence both for and against, 'we must balance the opposite experiments, where they are opposite, and deduct the smaller number from the greater' (*HR* 207). It is in this way that we balance evidence derived from human testimony. Where an event testified is an extraordinary one, we can say that the value of testimony diminishes in proportion as the fact is unusual. The incredibility of a fact can invalidate testimony even of the greatest authority.

A miracle, for Hume, is a violation of a law of nature: he gives as examples of miracles a dead man coming back to life and the raising of a house or ship into the air. Perhaps surprisingly, he does not deny that miracles are possible. His concern is not whether miracles can be done but whether they can be seen to be done. 'No testimony is sufficient to establish a miracle unless the testimony be of such a kind that its falsehood would be more miraculous than the fact, which it endeavours to establish' (*HR* 211). If someone tells me he saw a dead man restored to life, I must ask myself whether it is more probable that this person should either deceive or be deceived, or that the fact that he relates should really have happened. 'If the falsehood of his testimony would be more miraculous than the event which he relates; then, and not till then, can he pretend to command my belief or opinion' (*HR* 212).

Hume is not ruling out that a miracle could be proved, any more than he ruled out that a miracle could happen. Indeed, he tells us that given the appropriate unanimity of testimony, he would himself be prepared to believe what he regards as a miracle, namely a total darkness over the whole earth for eight days. We may find this surprising. If a miracle is a violation of the laws of nature, surely the evidence against it must always be stronger than the evidence against the frailty or malice of a witness. According to Hume's deterministic theory of human willing, however, a human action can be just as much a violation of a law of nature as any physical event.

The second part of the essay begins with a robust statement:

> There is not to be found, in all history, any miracle attested
> by a sufficient number of men, of such unquestioned

good-sense, education, and learning, as to secure us against
all delusion in themselves; of such undoubted integrity,
as to place them beyond all suspicion of any design to
deceive others; of such credit and reputation in the eyes
of mankind, as to have a great deal to lose in the case of
their being detected in any falsehood; and at the same time,
attesting facts performed in such a public manner and in
so celebrated a part of the world, as to render the detection
unavoidable: all which circumstances are requisite to give us
a full assurance in the testimony of men.   (*HR* 213)

Hume gives three arguments to back up this claim. First,
the human race is incorrigibly credulous, as is shown by the
number of fake miracles later discredited. Second, miracle
stories circulate mainly among ignorant and barbarous
nations; when, in reading history, 'we advance nearer the
enlightened ages', such stories become ever rarer. Third,
miracles are reported in favour of religions that contradict
each other. Hence any story of a miracle wrought in favour
of religion A must be a piece of evidence against religions B,
C and Z, and therefore against their alleged miracles.

To illustrate this last point Hume offers three examples.
In support of paganism there is a story in Tacitus of the
Emperor Vespasian curing with his spittle a man who was
blind and by his touch a man who was lame. In support of
Catholicism the sceptical Cardinal de Retz tells how a man
in Saragossa who had lost a leg grew a second one when
holy oil was applied to the stump. In support of the heresy of Jansenism, repeatedly condemned by popes, Hume
cites the miracles recently reported at the tomb of the Abbé
Paris, where 'The curing of the sick, giving hearing to the
deaf, and sight to the blind, were everywhere talked of as
the usual effects of that holy sepulchre.' These miracles, he

claims, were attested by credible witnesses, in the capital of France, 'the most eminent theatre that now is in the world' (*HR* 220).

Hume's picture is a little overdrawn and not quite consistent with his earlier point that miracles are only reported in barbarous contexts. None the less, the argument from the rival claims of incompatible religions does establish his case that a miracle cannot be proved in such a way as to be the foundation of a religion.

This conclusion does not in itself lead to atheism. No one had ever argued that it was the occurrence of miracles that proved the existence of God. But prior to the Enlightenment, many argued that if we know from elsewhere that there is a God who is almighty, then we can conclude that it is in his power to work miracles, perhaps in order to authenticate one sect rather than another.

Hume ends his essay by discounting as fabulous all the prodigies and miracles narrated in the Old Testament. He also attacks those who seek to defend Christianity with rational arguments: 'Our most holy religion is founded on Faith, not on reason.' The essay ends memorably:

> So that, upon the whole, we may conclude, that the Christian Religion not only was at first attended with miracles, but even at this day cannot be believed by any reasonable person without one. Mere reason is insufficient to convince us of its veracity: And whoever is moved by Faith to assent to it, is conscious of a continued miracle in his own person, which subverts all the principles of his understanding, and gives him a determination to believe what is most contrary to custom and experience. (*HR* 266)

Any reader of that passage today will be convinced that Hume is expressing, in an ironical form, his conviction that Christianity is so absurd and unreasonable that it is astonishing that anyone can believe it. However, not all his first readers took it that way. Irony of this kind was popular among the enlightenment masters of style, from Voltaire to Gibbon, and for good reason. In the climate of the time, such a use of irony was not just a mischievous frolic, it also provided a form of self-defence against dunderheaded orthodoxy. If a censorious divine alleged that the essay was anti-Christian, Hume could reply: 'Did I not say explicitly that Christianity was, from the start, attended with miracles?' If it was complained that he said it took a miracle to make anyone believe, he could reply: 'Don't you say yourself that faith is impossible without divine grace?'

Another device used by enlightenment thinkers to distance themselves from the unorthodox views they expressed was to make use of dialogue. Hume adopts this in the essay immediately following in *An Enquiry Concerning Human Understanding*, entitled 'Of a particular Providence and of a future State'. This contends that we can know nothing about God beyond the fact that he is the cause of the world, in particular that we cannot look forward to a future life in which the injustices of the present life will be redressed. But this argument is placed in the mouth of a friend improvising an address from the Greek philosopher Epicurus to the Athenian assembly.

4

Voltaire the man of letters

In 1750 Voltaire took up residence in Berlin as Chamberlain to Frederick II of Prussia. The appointment may seem surprising, its acceptance even more so. Since his accession ten years earlier, the King had hardly behaved like an enlightened monarch. He began his reign by invading the territories of his neighbour, the Empress Maria Theresa, thereby launching a frightful war, waged throughout Europe and beyond its boundaries. Voltaire, on the other hand, was not yet famous as the champion of liberty and the foe of orthodoxy. He was best known as a poet and playwright. After completing in 1711 his education at the Jesuit school of Louis-le-Grand, he adopted a literary career in place of the legal one for which his family had intended him. In 1717 he was imprisoned in the Bastille on the false charge of having written a satire on the Duke of Orleans, Prince Regent; this led him to change his birth name of Arouet for the pseudonym by which he is now universally known. In the following year his tragedy *Oedipus* was produced to great acclaim. Later, a quarrel with a nobleman led to a further term in the Bastille, followed by two years' exile in England, during which he published an epic poem in praise of Henri IV of France. This was followed by a life of Charles XII of Sweden and a series of successful dramas, such as *Zaire*, *Merope* and *Mahomet*. Though passages in these works, taken out of context, were used by critics to show that

Voltaire was already hostile to Christianity, the works as a whole were far from being revolutionary, and *Mahomet* was actually dedicated to Pope Benedict XIV.

It is true that Voltaire's *Lettres philosophiques*, in its commendation of Locke and Newton, its admiration of English political arrangements and its advocacy of the toleration of a proliferation of sects, foreshadowed much in his later philosophy. His enthusiasm for the minimalist religion of the Quakers gave an indication of the direction of his own theological thinking. The *Lettres*, when published in French in 1734 with the addition of an attack on the pessimistic theology of Pascal, was condemned by the Parlement of Paris and publicly burned. Thereupon Voltaire exiled himself to Cirey in Lorraine, where he lived for the next 15 years in the company of the scientifically erudite Mme du Châtelet. But prior to 1750 the furthest he had gone in challenging the authority of the Catholic Church was a poem attacking a parish priest for denying Christian burial to a famous actress who had refused to renounce her profession on her deathbed. In 1745 he even wrote a manifesto for the French soldiers who were intended to support Charles Edward Stuart's attempt to restore his dynasty in England.

It was not as reformer but as *littérateur* that Voltaire attracted Frederick II, who had aspirations himself in that area. The two men had already met more than once; they had discussed poetry a few years earlier, when Voltaire had been sent to Berlin by the French government on an abortive diplomatic mission. They wrote skittish compliments to each other in verse and in one letter Frederick addressed Voltaire as 'sublime spirit, firstborn of thinking beings'. The King was certainly capable of uttering impeccable enlightenment sentiments. With Voltaire's help he had published a treatise, *Anti-Machiavel*, against rapacity, perfidy, arbitrary government, unjust war and much else for which the King himself is now remembered.

The collaboration between the monarch and the philosopher did not last long. Frederick was not to be guided by the principles he professed, and Voltaire was oversensitive to any perceived insult to his genius. At the court he encountered another French enlightenment figure, Pierre Maupertuis (1698–1759), then President of the Berlin Academy. Unlike Voltaire, Maupertuis was a practising scientist, a Fellow of the Royal Society, who had earlier been sent to Lapland by King Louis XV to make exact measurements of a degree of latitude. His results, published in 1738, confirmed a conjecture of Newton's that the surface of the earth flattens towards the poles. The two court *philosophes* quarrelled, and Voltaire wrote a satiric diatribe about Maupertuis entitled *Doctor Akakia*. He published the text in spite of being forbidden to do so by Frederick, and he was forced to leave Prussia. At Frankfurt he was placed under house arrest for having carried off a book of the King's verses. No longer welcome in his own country either, he took up residence, after a year of travels, in a chateau in the territory of Geneva, then an independent city state politically resembling present-day Singapore. Henceforth his links with Frederick would be only epistolary.

In espousing Newton's physics, Voltaire had turned his back on the greatest natural philosopher of continental rationalism, Descartes. Now in the 1750s he shook off any allegiance he may have had to the greatest continental metaphysician of the age, G. W. Leibniz. In his *Theodicy* (a pseudo-Greek word coined to express the project of justifying the works of God to humankind), Leibniz had argued that in spite of appearances we live in the best of all possible worlds. His message was best known to English readers through its summary in Alexander Pope's *Essay on Man* (1734):

> Of Systems possible, if 'tis confest
> That Wisdom infinite must form the best ...
> Respecting Man, whatever wrong we call,
> May, must be right, as relative to all ...
> All Nature is but Art, unknown to thee:
> All Chance, Direction which thou canst not see;
> All Discord, Harmony, not understood;
> All partial Evil, universal Good:
> And, spite of Pride, in erring Reason's spite,
> One truth is clear, 'Whatever is, is RIGHT'.
>
> (Epistle I 43–4, 51–2, 289–94)

We do not know how far Voltaire ever accepted the optimistic metaphysics of Pope and Leibniz, to which he had been introduced by Frederick in 1737. In his tale *Zadig* of 1748, he had already questioned the idea that God's providence is exercised in an unjust world. What finally shocked him out of any such optimism was the Lisbon earthquake of 1755, which killed more than twenty thousand people. He wrote a poem on the subject entitled 'An Examination of the Axiom "All is Well"', which questioned whether the occurrence of such a disaster could be reconciled with the doctrine of an all-powerful and benevolent creator.

Voltaire's fullest response to the tragedy was his satirical novel *Candide* of 1759, in which the innocent young Candide is educated by Dr Pangloss, who instils in him two Leibnizian principles: the first is that everything has a sufficient reason; the other is that all is for the best in the best of all possible worlds. As Candide experiences expulsion from home, shipwreck, torture and the horrors of war, he continually repeats the mantras of Pangloss. He sustains his faith in them even while his beloved Cunégonde is raped and has her stomach slit open, and while Pangloss himself suffers the agonies of syphilis and is handed over to the Inquisition to be burned. Eventually, however, Candide cannot resist asking: 'If this is the best, what must the others be like?' and he finally renounces his philosophical optimism when he sees the cruelty meted out by a Dutch slave-owner to a negro in Surinam.

After a series of revolting adventures and improbable coincidences, Candide, Cunégonde and Pangloss, all much subdued, are reunited on a small farm in Turkey. The moral of the story is that rather than rely on philosophy or religion, human beings must settle down to simple work; for it is work that keeps away the three evils of boredom, vice and need. This teaching is memorably summarized in Candide's last words: 'We must cultivate our garden' (*C* 88).

5

The Encyclopedists

In 1751, shortly after Voltaire emigrated to Berlin, there appeared in Paris the first volume of the *Encyclopédie, ou Dictionnaire raisonné des sciences, des arts et des metiers,* edited by Denis Diderot and Jean d'Alembert. The ground for this project had been prepared for over half a century by earlier French thinkers. Pierre Bayle (1647–1706), for instance, in his *Dictionnaire Historique et Critique,* had shown, by detailed studies of biblical and historical personages, the inconsistency and incoherence of much of revealed theology. If religious faith was to be at all acceptable, Bayle argued, general toleration was essential. Belief in human immortality, or in the existence of God, was not something necessary for virtuous living, and therefore the teaching of ethics should be made independent of religious instruction.

The new *Encyclopédie* was similar in ethos but much vaster in scale. Its two editors were men of different talents and temperaments, the one more interested in physics and music, the other in the biological and social sciences. The two shared a faith in the inevitability of scientific progress, a belief that the Christian religion was a great obstacle to human betterment, and a fundamentally materialist view of human nature. Both men were combative in polemics, though one was more willing than the other to risk challenging authority.

Jean le Rond d'Alembert (1717–83) was the illegitimate son of a general, and was abandoned by his mother on the steps of the church of Saint-Jean-le-Rond in Paris, from which he received his name. Having studied both law and medicine, he devoted himself to mathematics and produced original work in fluid dynamics. While an exponent of experimental methods, he aimed to bring to all the sciences the clarity and accuracy of arithmetic and geometry. His first philosophical work was the introduction to the *Encyclopédie*, a manifesto of the ideal of a single great unified science. He maintained that if we knew how to take in the universe at a single view we would find it to be only one fact and one great truth. From the facts that all knowledge begins with the senses, and all humans have similar senses, he deduced that everyone was capable of mastering any science. The *Encyclopédie* itself was an expression of this belief in the power of universal education.

Denis Diderot (1713–84), the son of a cutler, was already a fluent linguist in his days at a Jesuit school, and started his publishing career with a series of translations from English. Before the *Encyclopédie* began to appear, he spent a period in prison in Vincennes because of publishing a *Letter on the Blind*. This questioned the existence of design in the universe, and contained a touching scene in which a blind professor on his deathbed confesses himself unable to see the world as an object of order and beauty.

Diderot emerged as editor in chief of the *Encyclopédie*, with d'Alembert taking responsibility for the mathematical parts. The two men gathered a group of like-minded thinkers as contributors to the *Encyclopédie*, including, besides Montesquieu and Voltaire, Julien de La Mettrie, a medical doctor who had recently published *L'Homme machine*, the

Baron d'Holbach, an atheist who presided over a lavish philosophical salon, and Claude Helvétius, a determinist psychologist who became notorious for a book arguing that human beings had no intellectual powers distinct from the senses.

From its earliest volumes the *Encyclopédie* made enemies by its anti-dogmatic and subversive tone. The Jesuits in particular attacked it, and after the second volume, and again after the seventh, it was suspended and suppressed by royal decree. Work on it continued in secret, though because some contributors – including Voltaire and d'Alembert – withdrew, the burden fell more and more on Diderot himself. The work eventually ran to seventeen volumes, of which the final ten appeared in 1766. By that time the Jesuits themselves had been suppressed, an event celebrated by d'Alembert in an anonymous tract.

The contributors to the *Encyclopédie* expressed their advanced views more cautiously in their contributions to the volumes than in their own works. This was especially true of Diderot himself, whose most important philosophical work, *D'Alembert's Dream*, was written in 1769. This consists of three linked dialogues. In the first, Diderot in conversation with d'Alembert introduces him to some novel ideas in biology. In the second, which gives its name to the triad, d'Alembert is asleep but talks aloud at length in the course of a dream. His companion, Mademoiselle de Lespinasse, is so struck by what she hears that she writes down the utterances, which she fears may be signs of madness. The medical doctor in attendance, Bordeu, assures her that the ideas of the sleeping mathematician are in fact plausible biological hypotheses, and goes on to supplement them with similar ideas of his own. Lespinasse makes her own shrewd contributions to the discussion, and eventually D'Alembert wakes up and joins in the conversation before going off to lunch. In the third and final dialogue, Bordeu and Lespinasse, left alone tête-à-tête, engage in a discussion of the morality of masturbation and miscegenation.

In the course of the three dialogues, the following propositions are presented:

1 The universe is a single physical system:

> There is only a single great individual, that is all. Within this whole, as within a machine or any animal, there are parts to which you give one or other name; but if you call a part of the whole an individual, it is under a misconception, as if you were to call a wing, or a feather in a wing, an individual.
>
> (*RA* 104)

The universe is made up of molecules of matter no two of which are alike but all of which are endowed with both sensitivity and motion.

2 There is no impassable gulf between the inorganic and the organic, between plants and animals, and between animals and humans. Even a genius like d'Alembert himself has developed, by insensible stages, from molecules cavorting in the bodies of his mother and father.

3 In humans there is not the great chasm between sensation and reason that philosophers had thought: 'there is a much greater distance between a chunk of marble and a sentient being than between a being with sensation and a being with thought' (*RA* 59). No supernatural agent is needed to account for the emergence of reason: 'from inert matter, organized in a certain way and impregnated with other inert matter, and given heat and motion, there

results sensation, life, memory, consciousness, passion, and thought' (*RA* 68).

In his description of the development and capacities of human beings, Diderot draws copiously on recent medical experience, citing descriptions of conjoined twins and of the recovery of trepanned patients. Each organ of the body has its own life, and the whole body moves as a unity in the same way as a swarm of bees. 'There is only one consciousness in an animal, but there is an infinity of wills: each organ has its own' (*RA* 138). The organs are all connected through a system of fibres to the central controlling organ, the brain, of which thought is no more than an operation. What is essential to thought and consciousness is memory: abstractions are mere linguistic signs to speed up discourse, and they are misleading if they are taken as representations of reality. Free will is an illusion: will is simply the latest impulse of desire and aversion, the last result of all that has been from birth to the present moment.

D'Alembert's Dream is a fascinating work but it is difficult to know how many of the ideas floated in it were seriously meant as scientific proposals. Bordeu describes the dream as 'systematic'; that is, as an unconfirmed hypothesis. He goes on to say that he believes 'the more human knowledge progresses, the more it will be verified' (*RA* 166). Considered as a prophecy, Diderot's text contains many remarkable successes and many near misses. However, the sequence of dialogues and the variety of characters provide many levels of distance between author and reader. At any given moment, who is speaking to us: Diderot the author, Diderot the character, d'Alembert asleep, d'Alembert awake, Bordeu or Lespinasse? The interposition of veils in this way was a device often used by enlightenment writers, no doubt as a method of self-defence against censors and inquisitors. But in this case Diderot seems to have felt that the precaution was insufficient, and he decided not to publish it. The book saw the light of day only after the French Revolution.

Towards the end of his life Diderot was a contributor to *A Philosophical History of the Two Indies*, which contained a passionate denunciation of imperialism and slavery. In 1773 he went to Russia to express his gratitude to Empress Catherine the Great, who nine years earlier had bought the reversion of his library and assigned him a pension for life. But his views on religion and sovereignty soon brought him into conflict with her, and he retired to France for the last ten years of his life. Catherine cannot have been pleased when he told her that the only true sovereign was the nation and that there could be no true legislator other than the people.

6

The birth of aesthetics

It was unusual for any of the major figures of the Enlightenment to be a university professor. Rather than compose treatises or textbooks, the *philosophes* preferred to write dialogues, fables or drama. It is fitting, therefore, that one of the academic ventures of the Enlightenment was the philosophical study of art and beauty, the discipline given the name 'aesthetics' by the German philosopher Alexander Gottlieb Baumgarten in 1735. It was in Germany and Britain, rather than in France, that the earliest classics of aesthetics were written, and two figures who stand out are Gotthold Ephraim Lessing (1729–81) and Edmund Burke (1729–97).

Lessing was the son of a Lutheran pastor and he was initially destined for the Church. He forsook theology, however, and supported himself in the course of a literary career by acting as librarian to the Duke of Brunswick at Wolfenbüttel. Like the *philosophes*, he expressed his thoughts by preference in essays and dramas. His first publication was an essay written jointly with the Jewish philosopher Moses Mendelssohn entitled 'Pope a Metaphysician!' This, like Voltaire's *Candide*, was an attack on the facile optimism expressed in Pope's *Essay on Man*. It went on to argue also that philosophy and poetry should be kept sharply separate as being two different spiritual activities. While criticizing Pope, Lessing admired English literature: in drama he held up Shakespeare as a model rather than the French tragedians. His own first tragedy, *Miss Sara Sampson*, was a deliberate attempt at drama in the English manner.

Meanwhile initial efforts in the philosophy of aesthetics had been made in England. David Hume's essay 'Of the Standard of Taste', first published in 1742, aimed to show that even though beauty was a matter of sentiment, there could be objective assessments of it, because it could be ascertained, as a matter of fact, which persons were more skilled at judgements of taste. Hume went so far as to argue that taste was less subject to the vagaries of fashion than was science. 'Aristotle and Plato, Epicurus and Descartes, may successively yield to each other: but Terence and Virgil maintain an universal, undisputed empire over the minds of men' (*ET* 274). Clearly, by 'science' he meant philosophy, and philosophy of his own especial kind.

The most substantial aesthetic treatise to appear in these years was Edmund Burke's *Philosophical Inquiry into our Ideas of the Sublime and the Beautiful* (1757). Not only the beautiful but also the sublime, Burke claimed, can be the aim of art. Transparency is not an essential feature of great art: the imagination can be affected as much by what is obscurely hinted at as much as by what is clearly stated. While the appreciation of beauty is a form of love without desire, to feel something as sublime is to feel astonishment without fear. The feeling for the sublime was traced by Burke to the fears and horrors implicit in the original instinct for self-preservation. The paradigm of the feeling for beauty, he maintained, was a chaste appreciation of female perfection, and this showed that the feeling derives from the need for social contact and ultimately from the instinct to propagate the race.

Lessing, in 1766, took further his early attempt to define the peculiar characteristics of the different intellectual and aesthetic disciplines. He published a book entitled *Laocoon, or the Limits of Poetry and Painting*. The artistic effect of the description of the death of Laocoon in Virgil's *Aeneid* is quite different, he argued, from that of the famous classical statue in the Vatican. In each case the book assigns the poet a special, semi-prophetic role. Lessing's own major dramatic work, the comedy *Minna von Barnhelm*, appeared a year later.

In the 1770s Lessing extended his literary studies into the dangerous realm of biblical criticism. He treated the Bible not as an inspired text but criticized it in the same way he would have treated any other book. He was the first person to observe that the fourth Gospel was in a different category from the other three, all of which he believed to have derived from a single Aramaic original. He had been given a set of posthumous papers from the estate of the heterodox theologian Hermann Reimarus (1694–1768), from which he published a series of 'Anonymous Wolfenbüttel Fragments'.

These contained reflections on the impossibility of the crossing of the Red Sea as narrated in Exodus, on the absence throughout the Old Testament of a doctrine of human immortality, and on the inconsistencies in the New Testament accounts of the Resurrection of Jesus. The counter-arguments that Lessing provided to the criticisms were palpably and perhaps deliberately flimsy. The publications raised a storm of counter-attacks from orthodox Lutherans. He himself distinguished between 'the religion of Christ' – which he took to be a simple Jewish apocalyptic vision – and 'the Christian religion' of the Trinity and the sacraments, which he thought was manifestly contrary to reason.

Like the leaders of the French Enlightenment, Lessing was a passionate advocate of religious toleration. He gave fullest expression to this advocacy in his drama *Nathan the Wise* (1779).

This was a dialogue between three characters, Nathan a Jew, Saladin a Muslim and a Christian Knight Templar. The conclusion of the dialogue is that what is required of humankind is not adherence to dogma but sincerity, toler- ance and brotherly love. One reason offered for toleration is that the worth of a person does not depend on whether that person's beliefs are true but on how much trouble he or she has taken to attain the truth. This novel argument was presented in a vivid paragraph often quoted since:

> If God held all truth in his right hand and in his left the everlasting striving after truth, so that I should always and everlastingly be mistaken, and said to me, Choose, with humility I would pick on the left hand and say, Father, grant me that; absolute truth is for thee alone.   (*GW* xiii.23)

Lessing's most important philosophical work was *The Education of the Human Race* (1780). Its theme is that the human race, like the human individual, passes through different stages, to which different kinds of instruction are appropriate. The upbringing of a child is a matter of physical rewards and punishment: the childhood of the human race was the era before Christ and the Old Testament is as it were a primary-school text – even though it does not mention any afterlife. In our youth, educators offer us more spiritual rewards for good conduct: eternal rewards and punish- ments for an immortal soul. This corresponds to the period of history dominated by the Christian religion. However, the evidence for the divine origin of Christianity is uncompelling, even if some of the miracle stories are true. Even the strongest historical evidence about contingent facts, Lessing went on to argue, cannot justify any conclusion to necessary truths about matters of divinity. Revelation tells us nothing that reason could not, but merely facilitates our advance.

The Christian religion, therefore, can be no more than a stage in the education of the human race, and its dogmas can have no more than symbolic value. Human nature, come of age, must extract from Christianity a belief in the universal family of humankind and must pursue moral values for their own sake, not for the sake of any reward here or hereafter.

Lessing was an admirer of Spinoza, whom he regarded as the only true philosopher. Like him, he regarded the world as a single unified system whose components were identical with ideas in the mind of God. He was willing to accept that determinism was true and that freedom was an illusion; on the other hand, he was willing to admit contingency in the world, with the consequence that some among God's ideas were contingent also. Lessing praised Spinoza for realizing that liberation from anxiety is only to be achieved by accepting the inevitability of destiny.

7

Jean-Jacques Rousseau

In 1750s the Enlightenment welcomed into its nest a gigantic cuckoo. Born in Geneva in 1712, the son of a widower watchmaker, Jean-Jacques Rousseau was brought up a Calvinist but at the age of 16, a runaway apprentice to an engraver, he became a Catholic in Turin. This was at the instigation of the Baronne de Warens, with whom he lived at Annecy in Savoy for periods between 1729 and 1740. After short spells as a singing master and a household tutor, he went to Paris in 1742, bearing with him a new system of musical notation that he hoped might make his fortune. Failing in this project, he obtained a year later a post as secretary to the French ambassador in Venice. Dismissed for insubordination, he returned to Paris, where he became close to Diderot, whom he visited regularly during his imprisonment. He was also for a while on good terms with d'Alembert and Voltaire. In 1752 he attracted public notice with his opera *The Village Soothsayer*, which was produced before Louis XV at Fontainebleau to considerable acclamation.

Rousseau contributed to the *Encyclopédie* several articles on musical and economic topics. However, he shocked the *philosophes* when in 1750 he published a prize essay that answered in the negative the question whether the progress of the arts and sciences had had a beneficial effect on morality. Four years later, he followed this up with a *Discourse on the Origin and Foundations of Inequality among Men.*

This explosive pamphlet begins with a history of the early stages of human development and devotes many pages to the question whether language produced society or society produced language. These pages set out clearly the difficulties that attend any scientific account of the origin of language; difficulties that, exactly as he predicted, have still not been overcome, centuries after he wrote.

The main theme of the work is that humanity was naturally good, and has been corrupted by social institutions. Savages at the present time are already at some distance from the state of nature, but the ideal human being was the 'noble savage', whose simple goodness put civilized humanity to shame. 'The state of nature is the one in which man's concern for his survival least encroaches on that of others, it is the one most conducive to peace and befitting of mankind' (*DI* 44). Inequalities of rank and wealth, Rousseau argued, were the inevitable result of the process of civilization, which sacrificed natural needs and values in favour of a superficial intellectual culture. As culture became more splendid, human relationships became weaker and the individual became alienated from his or her real self. It is reason that turns people inward and isolates them from other people and natural pity for their fate. 'Some one may with impunity slit the throat of a fellow man under the philosopher's window.' (*DI* 47)

All this was at the opposite pole from the Encyclopedists' faith in scientific and social progress: Voltaire called the *Discourse* 'a book against the human race'. Rousseau struck back at the *philosophes* with a *Letter to D'Alembert* in 1758. In an article on 'Geneva' in the seventh volume of the *Encyclopédie*, d'Alembert had regretted that there was no theatre in the city. Rousseau responded that a theatre in

Geneva would only corrupt a society that, by comparison with a metropolis such as Paris, was still sufficiently close to nature to be unspoiled. All sound entertainment, he argued, must be an integral part of people's working life, and not an artificial charade that, among other things, debased the role of women.

It was not, however, as if Rousseau himself was a model of traditional family life. He exhibited his contempt for social convention by a long-standing liaison with a washerwoman, Thérèse Levasseur. By her he had five children, whom he dumped, one after the other, in a foundling hospital. In 1754 he had returned to Geneva and converted back to Calvinism in order to regain citizenship there. Voltaire, having returned from Berlin, had now settled in the Geneva region, but the two philosophers were not destined to be good neighbours. Their mutual distaste became public with Rousseau's *Letter on Providence*, published in 1756. Rousseau had already quarrelled with Diderot for leaking an amatory confidence, and his break with the *philosophes* was complete when he published his *Lettres morales* of 1761.

The years 1758 to 1761 were very productive for Rousseau, who spent the period in retirement in a small French country house. He wrote a novel, *Julie, ou La Nouvelle Héloïse*, which was an immediate bestseller when it appeared in Paris in 1761. He also wrote a philosophical treatise on education entitled *Émile*, which narrated the life of a child educated as an experiment in isolation from other children. Despite containing an eloquent profession of faith in natural religion, this book was swiftly condemned in Geneva and by the Archbishop and by the Parlement of Paris.

In the same year, 1762, Rousseau published his most influential work on political philosophy, *The Social Contract*. It opens with the memorable words 'Man is born free, and he is everywhere in chains.' This beginning might make us expect that the chains are those of social institutions and that we are about to be encouraged to reject the social order. Instead we are told that membership of society is a sacred right that is the basis of all other rights. Social institutions, Rousseau now thinks, liberate rather than enslave.

In a state of nature, according to Rousseau, a human has only simple, animal desires: 'the only goods he acknowledges in the world are food, a female, and sleep; the only ills he fears are pain and hunger' (*SC* 4.2). In this state humans are not necessarily hostile to each other, for these desires are not inherently competitive. They are motivated by self-love, to be sure, but self-love can be combined with sympathy and compassion for one's fellows.

In a state of nature there are no property rights and therefore neither justice nor injustice. But as society develops from its primitive state, the lack of such rights begins to be felt. Economic co-operation and technical progress make it necessary to form an association for the protection of individuals' persons and possessions. How can this be done while allowing each member of the association to remain as free as before? The *Social Contract* provides the solution by presenting the concept of the general will.

The general will comes into existence when each person submits to the supreme direction of the general will (*SC* 1.6). This compact creates a public person, a moral and collective body, the state or sovereign people. Every individual is both a sovereign and a subject: as a citizen he or she shares in the sovereign authority, and as a subject owes obedience to the laws of the state. The sovereign has no existence or interest independent of the contracting citizens who compose it: it expresses the general will and it cannot go wrong in its pursuit of the public good.

But what is the general will, and how is it to be ascertained? It is not the same as the unanimous will of the citizens: Rousseau distinguished between 'the general will' and 'the will of all'. 'There is often considerable difference between the will of all and the general will. The latter is concerned only with the common interest, the former with interests that are partial, being itself but the sum of particular wills' (*SC* 3.3). Should we say then that the general will should be identified with the will of the majority of the citizens? No, the deliberations of a popular assembly are by no means infallible: voters may suffer from ignorance or be swayed by individual self-interest.

The general will can be determined by plebiscite but only on two conditions: first, every voter must be fully informed; and second, no two voters may communicate with each other, lest groups be formed that are smaller than the whole community. Not only political parties but religious groups also must be banned if the general will is to find expression in a referendum. It is only within the context of the entire community that the differences between the self-interest of individuals will cancel out and yield the self-interest of the sovereign people as a whole.

Rousseau is no devotee of the principle of separation of powers. The sovereignty of the people, he says, is indivisible: if you separate the powers of the legislative and executive branches, you make the sovereignty chimerical. However, the sovereign people should legislate only on very general matters, leaving executive power concerning particular issues in the hands of government. But the government must always act as a delegate of the people, and ideally a popular assembly should meet at regular intervals to confirm the constitution and renew or terminate the mandate of the holders of public office.

The type of arrangement here proposed by Rousseau seems practicable only in a Swiss canton or a city-state like Geneva. But like Montesquieu, he insisted that one cannot specify a single form of government as appropriate to all circumstances. But what, in a Rousseauian state, are the rights of dissident minorities? The social compact, according to Rousseau, tacitly includes an undertaking that whoever refuses to submit to it may be constrained by his fellow citizens to conform to it. 'This means nothing other than that he shall be forced to be free' (*SC* 1.7). If I vote against a measure that then triumphs in a poll, this shows I was mistaken about where my true good, and my genuine freedom, were to be found.

In spite of his concern with the general will, Rousseau was not a wholehearted supporter of democracy in practice. 'If there were a people of gods, they would govern themselves democratically. But a government of such perfection is not suitable for human beings' (*SC* 3.4). He believed that direct democracy would be fractious and inefficient. Better have an elective aristocracy in which the wise govern the masses: 'there is no point in getting twenty thousand men to do what a hundred select men can do ever better' (*SC* 3.4).

This seems a tame and bourgeois conclusion to a book that began by calling humankind to throw off its chains. None the less, the concept of the general will had an explosive revolutionary potential. Examined closely, the notion is theoretically incoherent and practically vacuous. It is not true as a matter of logic that if A wills A's good and B wills B's good then A and B jointly will the good of A and B:

the goods of each may not be compatible with each other. This remains true, however well informed A and B may be, because there may be a genuine, unavoidable incompatibility between the goods of each.

Though its revolutionary potential took some time to take effect, the book was instantly viewed as dangerous. With a warrant out for his arrest in both Geneva and Paris, Rousseau fled to Switzerland (of which Geneva was not at that time a part). After seeking refuge in various continental cities he was, as we shall see, eventually given sanctuary in England through the good offices of David Hume.

8

Reason and sentiment

The period of the Enlightenment has often been called 'The Age of Reason'. Whether the appellation is appropriate depends on what is being contrasted with reason: is it faith or is it emotion? The Enlightenment certainly exalted the role of unaided human reason in contrast to the claims of sacred texts and alleged revelations. But in matters of morals it was a key element of enlightenment thought that morality derived rather from an emotion or set of emotions.

Reason had already been dethroned within ethics by Hume in his youthful *Treatise*. Reason itself, he told us there, is impotent to produce any action: what motivates voluntary behaviour is passion. Passion can never be overcome by reason but only by a contrary passion. 'Reason is and ought only to be the slave of the passions, and can never pretend to any other office than to serve and obey them' (*T* 415). Since reason cannot move us to action, moral judgements cannot be the product of reason because the whole purpose of such judgements is to guide our behaviour. Reason is concerned either with relations of ideas or with matters of fact, but neither of these leads on to action. Only the passions can do that, and reason can neither cause nor judge our passions: ''Tis not contrary to reason to prefer the destruction of the whole world to the scratching of my finger' (*T* 416).

All that reason can do is to determine the feasibility of the objects sought by the passions and the best methods of achieving them. The chief source of moral distinctions is not reason but rather the feeling of sympathy with others. Justice is approved of because it tends to the public good; and the public good means nothing to us, except in so far as sympathy interests us in it. 'Virtue is consider'd as a means to an end. Means to an end are only valued so far as the end is valued. But the happiness of strangers affects us by sympathy alone' (*T* 577).

Hume's emphasis on the role of sympathy as a fundamental element in our moral judgements was carried further by Adam Smith. Unusually for a *philosophe*, Smith was a university professor, who held chairs of logic and moral philosophy at Glasgow University. In 1759 he published a *Theory of Moral Sentiments*, which presented a complex analysis of sympathy itself and of its relationship to morality. Sympathy, we are told, arises from imagination, not from sensation:

> though our brother is upon the rack, as long as we ourselves are at our ease, our senses will never inform us of what he suffers . . . it is by changing places in the fancy with the sufferer that we come either to conceive or to be affected by what he feels. (*TMS* 10)

Imagination, indeed, can enable us to feel for another in ways of which he himself is incapable: thus 'we blush for the impudence and rudeness of another, though he himself appears to have no sense of the impropriety of his own behaviour' (*TMS* 12).

Whereas, for Hume, sympathy was essentially a sharing of pleasure or pain with another, for Smith sympathy has a broader scope and can arise from the sharing of any passion. Agreeably, Smith often illustrates this in the case of the passion of merriment, as when people share a joke. More seriously, our concern for justice arises from sympathy with a victim's resentment of harm. Our approval of benevolence arises from sympathy both with the benefactor's generosity and with the beneficiary's gratitude. We make judgements of the propriety or impropriety of conduct on the basis of sympathizing or not sympathizing with the person in question:

> When we judge in this manner of any affection, as proportioned or disproportioned to the cause which excites it, it is scarce possible that we should make use of any other rule or canon but the correspondent affection in ourselves.
>
> (*TMS* 18)

Smith makes a distinction between virtue and propriety. Propriety is a basic level of morality: it concerns actions that deserve approval but not admiration. Virtue is more exalted: it is exhibited in actions that deserve to be celebrated. Eating when we are hungry is perfectly proper, but it would be absurd to call it virtuous. Smith's standard of propriety is somewhat austere: to cry out with pain is always unmanly and unbecoming, and gout and toothache deserve no sympathy. Grief must not be huddled in solitude: a bereaved person must return as soon as possible to the daylight of society.

Humans all desire the respect and admiration of others. Two roads to this goal present themselves: on the one hand the study of wisdom and the practice of virtue, on the other the acquisition of wealth and greatness. Fortunately, in many stations of life, so Smith believed, the road to virtue and that to fortune are very nearly the same. 'In all the middling and inferior professions, real and solid professional abilities, joined to prudent, just, firm and temperate conduct, can very seldom fail of success' (*TMS* 63). Sadly, the same is not true when we move above the middle classes to the drawing rooms of the great and the courts of princes. The tendency to admire the rich and great, and to despise the poor and mean, is the source of a great corruption of moral sentiments.

Moral judgement, Smith insists, is essentially a social enterprise: a person brought up on a desert island 'could no more think of his own character, of the propriety or demerit of his own sentiments and conduct, of the beauty or deformity of his own mind than of the beauty or deformity of his own face' (*TMS* 110). We need the mirror of society to show us ourselves. Because our first moral judgements are made about the character and conduct of other people, we cannot form any judgement of our own sentiments or motives unless we can somehow distance ourselves from them. Hence:

> I divide myself, as it were, into two persons . . . The first
> is the spectator, whose sentiments with regard to my own
> conduct I endeavour to enter into, by placing myself in his
> situation, and by considering how it would appear to me,
> when seen from that particular point of view. The second
> is the agent, the person whom I properly call myself, and
> of whose conduct, under the character of a spectator, I was
> endeavouring to form some opinion. (*TMS* 113)

This character, the impartial spectator thus introduced into ethics, was to make a frequent appearance in the pages of subsequent moral philosophers.

Smith does not appeal to any revelation as the source of morality, but when he comes to discuss the role of duty he does invoke God as a kind of supreme impartial spectator. General rules, he tells us, are justly regarded as divine laws. The sense of duty is important because quite often we fail to feel the sentiment that sympathy would dictate. A man may be deficient in feeling gratitude to a benefactor, and yet take every opportunity to make a proper return for his services. A wife:

> may sometimes not feel that tender regard for her husband which is suitable to the relation that subsists between them. If she has been virtuously educated, however, she will endeavour to act as if she felt it, to be careful, officious, faithful and sincere. (*TMS* 162)

Without the sense of duty that makes us pay sacred regard to general rules, no one can be relied on. The necessary reverence for them, we are told, is enhanced by an opinion first impressed by nature, and later confirmed by philosophy, that these rules of morality are the commands and laws of the Deity, who will finally reward the obedient and punish the transgressors. Our moral faculties are, as it were, vice-gerents God has set up within us.

Though Smith places a high value on the effect on behaviour of the popular belief in immortality, it is not altogether clear how far he shares the belief himself. And while proclaiming that it is right to place a double confidence in the behaviour of a religious person, he insists that this is so only:

> wherever men are not taught to regard frivolous observances as more immediate duties of religion than acts of justice and beneficence and to imagine that by sacrifices and ceremonies and vain supplications they can bargain with the Deity for fraud and perfidy and violence. (*TMS* 170)

Indispensable though the sense of duty is, Smith tells us that it is wrong to think that it should be the sole motive of our conduct. The actions to which we are prompted by the benevolent affections should be motivated not by obedience to rule but by the passions themselves. Not so with regard to the malevolent passions: we should punish from a sense of propriety rather than from any savage disposition to revenge. The extent to which our conduct should be regulated by rules varies from case to case. Justice determines with exactness what is required from case to case, but the actions required by friendship, humanity, hospitality are vague and indeterminate. 'The rules of justice may be compared to the rules of grammar; the rules of the other virtues to the rules which critics lay down for the attainment of what is sublime and elegant in composition' (*TMS* 175).

9

Voltaire as philosopher

Adam Smith concludes his treatment of duty with a consideration of the way mistaken religious ideas can distort moral judgement. To illustrate this he refers to Voltaire's tragedy *Mahomet*, which he regarded as 'the very climax of dramatic excellence'. In 1759, the year Smith's book appeared, Voltaire's life had taken a new turn. He had just moved into a chateau at Ferney, on the shore of Lake Geneva but actually in French territory, where he remained almost until his death in 1778. His endeavours during that period were mainly devoted to the writing of philosophy and to the pursuit of justice rather than to the production of drama, though he built a theatre beside his house where there were often amateur performances of his earlier plays.

At Ferney, Voltaire lived a quiet life, taking good care of his tenants and neighbours, and far removed from the courts of Paris and Berlin. He continued, however, to be a figure of international repute. Many of the great figures of the age made the pilgrimage to Ferney: James Boswell, for instance, and Dr Charles Burney. And though he was banished from Paris he remained a subject of interest at the court. Louis XV's mistress, Madame de Pompadour, went so far as to propose that he be given a Cardinal's hat.

In 1761 a young Protestant, Marc-Antoine Calas, was found dead in his father's house in Toulouse. It was alleged that he had been killed by his father, Jean Calas, to prevent him converting to Catholicism. Jean was tortured to make him confess to the crime, and condemned to death, despite maintaining his innocence right up to his execution on the wheel. Supported by leading Calvinists, a member of the family travelled to Ferney and persuaded Voltaire to take up the dead man's cause. This he did with energy and courage, notably by circulating a *Treatise on Tolerance* in 1763. Two years later the Toulouse verdict was overturned at Versailles, and it was established that Marc-Antoine had committed suicide. Voltaire wrote up the story and made it the framework of the final published version of the *Treatise*.

This powerful work is not at all an attack on religion or even on Catholicism; rather, it argues against religious fanaticism on religious grounds. 'We have enough religion to hate and persecute, and we have not enough to love and help', Voltaire complains at the outset, and he concludes the work with an eloquent prayer to God: 'You did not give us a heart to hate each other, nor hands to cut each other's throats: make us rather help each other to bear the burden of our painful and transitory life' (*TT* 141).

The basis of human law is the principle 'do not do to others what you would not want others to do to you', but it has been replaced in some Catholic countries, he complains, with 'Believe what I believe, and what you cannot believe, or you will die.' He gives a vivid narrative of the wars of religion that followed the Reformation, and he contrasts the intolerance of Europe with the tolerance of the Ottoman and Chinese Empires.

In a long and uneven historical section, Voltaire argues that intolerance was unknown to the ancient Greeks and Romans. The number of Christian martyrs in the Roman

Empire has been much exaggerated, he claims, and those who were actually executed were not necessarily put to death for their religion. He labours to show that the Hebrew Bible provides no authorization for intolerance, and on firmer ground he points out that in late Judaism, Pharisees and Sadducees did not feel obliged to execute each other. The evangelists and apostles, notably Saints Peter and Paul, disagreed with each other without feeling they needed to go to war with each other. 'I say with horror, but with truth, it is us Christians, it is we who have been persecutors, executioners, murderers' (*TT* 80).

In the *Treatise* Voltaire proclaims himself a good Catholic, and occasionally at Ferney he received the sacraments, to the scandal of his *philosophe* friends. But he mocks the subtlety and sophistry of some of the dogmas proclaimed in the history of the Church: 'Less dogmas, less disputes; less disputes, less misery', he says. He attacks the cruelty of the way doctrines are enforced, representing a confessor as saying to a dying man that if he will not subscribe to the definitions of the Council of Nicaea, 'I will throw your body into the sewer, your wife will lose her dowry, and your family will beg in vain for bread.'

In spite of the passion with which it is written, the *Treatise* proposes only a modest degree of toleration for French Calvinists. They are to be treated in the way Roman Catholics are treated in England: allowed to practise their religion but subject to fines and excluded from public office. Voltaire is willing to accept the dictum 'There is no salvation outside the Church', but he says that to claim that all who are not Roman Catholics are destined to damnation is to usurp the right of God alone to determine the eternal fate of the millions of the rest of the world.

In the course of the Calas dispute, Voltaire became gradually more hostile to Catholicism and to Christianity in general. Already in 1722 in a poem addressed to God, he had declared: 'I am not a Christian that I may love thee more'; but for many years he denied authorship of this poem. He began to make his views public in *A Philosophical Dictionary*, first published in pocket form in 1764. Many an entry contains, sometimes thinly disguised by irony, sometimes pseudonymously attributed, an attack on contemporary church teaching and practice. Under the heading 'Credo', Voltaire places in the mouth of a fictional Abbé a creed that among others contains the following articles:

> I believe that it is our duty to regard all men as our brothers since God is our common father.
> I believe that the persecutor is abominable and that he ranks immediately after the poisoner and the parricide.
> I believe that theological disputes are at once the world's most ridiculous farce and most frightful scourge, immediately after war, pestilence, famine and the pox.
> I believe that monks must be absolutely exterminated.
> (*PD* 161)

Voltaire continued to hold in honour the person of Jesus, though he regarded as absurd the idea that any human could be God incarnate. It was the moral teacher, not the miracle worker, whom he revered. He insisted that Jesus taught no metaphysical dogmas: he did not say that he was consubstantial with the father, or that he had two wills and two natures. He left it to the Dominicans and Franciscans, 1,200 years later, to argue whether his mother was conceived in original sin. He instituted neither monks nor inquisitors; he commanded nothing of what we see today: (*PD* 173) 'The catholic, apostolic and Roman religion is the opposite of the religion of Jesus in all its ceremonies and in all its dogmas' (*PD* 393).

In his dictionary, in the article 'Atheism', Voltaire addresses the question raised by Bayle, whether a society of atheists could hold together. Are men held in check only by fear of a vengeful God who will punish, in this life or the next, human injustice? His answer is equivocal. It is, he says, infinitely more useful in a civilized city to have a bad religion than none at all, but on the other hand, fanaticism is a thousand times more baneful than atheism. His ultimate conclusion is that atheism is a monstrous evil in those who govern and also in learned men even if their lives are innocent (*PD* 57). Famously, he said that if God did not exist it would be necessary to invent him.

There is no doubt that Voltaire himself believed in God: he described himself as a theist, and in his dictionary a theist is defined as:

> a man firmly convinced of the existence of a supreme being as good as he is powerful, who has created all extended, vegetating, sentient and thinking beings, who perpetuates their species, who punishes crimes without cruelty, and benevolently rewards virtuous behaviour. (*PD* 386)

I find it hard to decide whether Voltaire believed in an afterlife. In the article 'Soul' he insists that the doctrine of immortality was unknown in the Old Testament and says that 'it is only by revelation that we can know the nature and destination of the soul'. He mocks the teaching of theologians and philosophers concerning the soul's survival after death, how the soul:

> will hear without ears, smell without a nose, and touch without hands; which body it will afterwards resume, the

one it had at the age of two or at eighty; how I, the identity of the same person, will subsist; how the soul of a man become imbecile, and dead imbecile at the age of seventy, will pick up the thread of the ideas it had at the age of puberty. (*PD* 24)

This passage seems to confuse two different dogmas – the immortality of the soul and the resurrection of the body – and it was much criticized at the time, notably by James Boswell when he visited Ferney. He recorded their conversation:

BOSWELL   Your philosophical dictionary troubles me. For instance, your article on the soul.

VOLTAIRE   That is a good article.

BOSWELL   No, excuse me. Is it [immortality] not a pleasing imagination? Is it not more noble?

VOLTAIRE   Yes. You have a noble desire to be King of Europe. I wish it, and I ask your protection. But it is not probable.

Later, Voltaire wrote to Boswell:

You seem solicitous about that pretty thing called Soul. I do not protest you, I know nothing of it, nor whether it is, nor what it is, nor what it shall be. Young scholars and priests know all that perfectly. For my part, I am but a very ignorant fellow. (*BGT* 293; 310)

In the course of his quarrels with ecclesiastical authority, Voltaire adopted the slogan *Écrasez l'infâme* – 'Crush the whore'. The whore was not religion as such – it was rather the superstition, bigotry and fanaticism he believed to be characteristic of the Church of his time. As he put it in the *Treatise on Tolerance*: 'Superstition is to religion what astrology is to astronomy, the crazy daughter of a wise mother' (*TT* 129).

In 1778 Voltaire returned to Paris for the first night of his last play, *Irène*. Though King Louis XVI remained suspicious of him, the people of the capital gave him a triumphant welcome, and he died in the glow of popular acclaim.

10

A quarrel between friends

While Voltaire had been turning himself from a poet-
ical dramatist into a philosopher, David Hume had been
undergoing a transformation in a different direction, from
philosopher to historian. He had been deeply impressed by
The Spirit of the Laws in 1748 and began a correspondence
with Montesquieu. He had part of that book published in
Edinburgh and decided to become a historian himself. He
quickly absorbed the theory that the course of history was
the product of an organic society. But it was not until 1754
that the first volume of his *History of England* appeared, and
he began the story in the middle, with the reigns of James I
and Charles I. Later volumes took the story forwards to the
revolution of 1688 and backward from the Tudor period to
Julius Caesar's invasion of Britain in 45 BC. The series was
brought to an end in 1761.

While Hume's historical method followed the best practice of the Enlightenment, his narrative history did not
share the Enlightenment's approval of the Whig settlement
of the British constitution. The first volume described the
early Stuart monarchy as a golden age, and treated the Civil
War as an unnecessary turmoil caused by Scottish fanaticism. As later volumes appeared, Hume went so far as to
revise this first in order to remove what he called 'the plaguy
prejudices of whiggism with which I was too much infected
when I began this work' (*L* i.379). What is the explanation

of this? It was that the Whig interpretation of the constitution was based on an a priori theory of constitution,
derived from Locke. Already in his essay 'Of the Protestant
Succession' of 1748, Hume offered purely local and prag-
matic reasons for preferring Hanoverian rule to that of the
Stuarts (with whose cause, incidentally, he had sympathized
until the rebellion of 1745). Hume's arguments fit well with
Montesquieu's insistence on the influence of environment
on society.

Whig constitutional theory was supported by a Whig
account of history. According to that, the English, since the
time of the Anglo-Saxon kings, had enjoyed certain liberties on which tyrannical kings had encroached from time
to time, but which were now everlastingly entrenched in the
Hanoverian constitutional monarchy. In his history, Hume
set out to show that this was a legend and that a strong
monarchy had often been the protector of the lower classes
against the depredations of the wealthy noblemen who
were the ancestors and precursors of those who had made
the settlement of 1688. His own support for the House of
Hanover was based on two premises: first, that a hereditary
monarchy avoided the factionalism attendant on an elective
system; second, that the fact that the Georges were not the
lineal heirs to the throne made it clear that their monarchy
was the creation of a free people (*ET* 553).

Unlike his philosophical works, Hume's history was well
received in religious quarters: he was congratulated by
the Archbishops of Canterbury and York. In 1763 Hume
accompanied Lord Hertford to Paris and two years later
became secretary to the embassy there in 1765, acting for
some months as chargé d'affaires. He was warmly received
at the French court and met many of the French *philosophes*.

He found their company, and that of their ladyfolk, highly congenial. 'The men of letters here are really very agreeable all of them Men of the World, living in entire or almost entire Harmony among themselves, and quite irreproachable in their morals', he wrote to a clerical friend in Scotland, adding implausibly that 'there is not a single Deist among them'. After a while he learned better, and reported to the same correspondent the points in which Paris society differed from England: '[T]he general regard pay'd to Genius and Learning; the universal and profess'd, tho decent, Gallantry of the Fair Sex; and the almost universal contempt of all Religion, among both sexes and among all Ranks of Men' (*L* i.497).

Hume returned to England in 1766, taking with him Jean-Jacques Rousseau, who was anxious to seek sanctuary there. Persecution and attempts on his life had made it difficult for him to live in peace even in Switzerland. Rousseau had been brought to Hume's attention in 1762 by Madame de Boufflers, his chief female acquaintance in Paris. While expressing reservations in private about *Émile* and *The Social Contract*, Hume wrote to Rousseau 'of all men of Letters in Europe, since the Death of President Montesquieu, you are the person whom I most revere' (*L* i.364).

Rousseau's sojourn in London began well and Hume described him to a friend as 'a very modest, mild, well-bred, gentle spirited, and warm-hearted man'. He went to great trouble to make him comfortable in England, applying to the King to grant him a pension and finding accommodation for him in the wilderness of Derbyshire to satisfy his passion for solitude. But the prickly Rousseau was difficult to help. He attached impossible conditions to the receipt of his pension and took offence at the artifices Hume and his friends had adopted to conceal from him that they were funding his travel expenses. On receipt of a monstrously ungrateful letter from him, Hume lost patience, describing him now as 'the blackest and most atrocious Villain, beyond comparison, that now exists in the World' and publishing a pamphlet with an account of their quarrel. Rousseau fled back to France and devoted the rest of his life to writing the *Confessions* that he had begun in Derbyshire.

Before Hume had ever met Rousseau he had been warned against him by one of the most influential of the Paris thinkers, Paul d'Holbach. D'Holbach (1723–89) was a German who had taken French nationality and in 1753 inherited a barony from an uncle. He contributed many articles on natural sciences to the *Encyclopédie* and was a friend of Diderot and d'Alembert. His salon in Paris became the social centre of the French Enlightenment and he was nicknamed *le premier maître d'hôtel de la philosophie*. He and his wife also entertained intellectuals from overseas, including Hume, Smith, Franklin and Gibbon.

Of all the enlightenment figures, d'Holbach was the one most hostile to religion as well as the most outspoken champion of atheism. During the 1760s he circulated a number of anti-religious tracts with titles such as 'Christianity unmasked' and 'A critical history of Jesus Christ'. But it was his *System of Nature* of 1770 that was a comprehensive manifesto of materialistic atheism.

Materialism – the doctrine that everything including human life and thought is to be explained by the properties and motions of matter – had already in 1748 been given expression in the work *Man a Machine* by an early enlightenment thinker, Julien de La Mettrie (1709–51). Descartes had been famous for his teaching that animals were automata, while only humans had minds that could feel and think. La Mettrie took this mechanistic doctrine further: it was not only, as Descartes maintained, that the human body was a machine; so was the entire human being. There was no need to postulate a soul or mind: all forms of life and thought emerged simply from the motion of organized matter.

Materialism of this kind does not necessarily involve atheism. It was a favourite topic of discussion among enlightenment thinkers whether Locke was correct to speculate that God might be able to endow matter with thought. La Mettrie himself professed agnosticism about the existence of God. D'Holbach, however, on the basis of materialism, went on to proclaim the necessity of atheism. In the words of Diderot, he 'rained bombs upon the house of the Lord'.

The universe, according to d'Holbach, is composed of a multitude of atoms of various kinds, each with its characteristic motion. These atoms in motion are the sole cause of all phenomena, including human physical and mental phenomena. They act in accordance with fixed and necessary laws, so that whatever happens has been determined from all eternity. The things we encounter in experience are all different organizations of atoms, and their activities result from their particular structures. While the totality of matter remains constant, plants and animals are constantly changing, while seeking to preserve themselves in existence. Individuals come and go, emerging from, and returning to 'the universal storehouse' of nature.

Human beings too are organized structures of atoms, and their behaviour is determined by their physical constitution. Attraction and repulsion are ubiquitous in nature, and in humans they take the form of attraction to pleasure and aversion to pain. Humans, like other beings, seek to continue in existence, and the driving force of their actions is self-love – a self-love, however, that is compatible with a concern for other members of our society. All that is necessary for the understanding of human thought and behaviour will come from the study of the brain and the nervous system and the patterns of education.

The universe, d'Holbach tells us, has always existed and has no need of any supernatural being to create it. It is a tragedy that ignorant and fearful humans have created mythical deities as imaginary supports in their quest for happiness. No coherent account of divinity can be given, so that the word 'God' is a meaningless term. But the belief in God has falsified human nature and set men off on a fruitless quest for immortality. Religion, so far from being necessary for morality, is positively harmful to it. Atheism is essential for human progress and happiness.

The belligerent atheism of d'Holbach was too extreme for some of his enlightenment colleagues. Voltaire offered a detailed refutation of it in a later edition of his *Dictionary*, and Frederick the Great wrote a critical analysis of the *System of Nature*. As d'Holbach wrote in his own later work, *Good Sense*: 'He who combats religion . . . resembles a man who uses a sword to kill fruit-flies . . . as soon as the blow is struck, the fruit flies return.' But as the Enlightenment progressed, many others followed d'Holbach on the slope that leads from deism, through scepticism, to atheism.

11

Transatlantic enlightenment

Benjamin Franklin (1706–90) was the youngest son of a Boston tallow-chandler who was the father of 17 children. In his engaging *Autobiography* he tells us that he had only two years' schooling before being apprenticed as a printer, at the age of 12, to his elder brother James. In his teens he succeeded James as editor of a newspaper, the *New England Courant*, which enjoyed a reputation for sedition. Before long he departed for Philadelphia, where he was befriended by the governor of Pennsylvania, who offered to set him up on his own as a printer.

In 1724 Franklin went to England and spent 18 months learning the latest printing techniques and technology. Back in Philadelphia he rapidly became the city's most successful printer. He set up the city's first police force and first fire-insurance company, and founded its first hospital. He promoted street cleaning and lighting, himself perfecting a new type of ventilated lantern. Having established America's first circulating library, he went on to be one of the founders of the American Philosophical Society on the model of the English Royal Society. Finally, he set up an academy, which is today the University of Pennsylvania.

Alongside these civic endeavours, Franklin continued his own lifelong education. He taught himself French, Latin, Italian and Spanish. By 1725 he had worked out his own religious position. He disowned the doctrines of grace and predestination and ceased to believe in immortality. He adopted a form of deism similar to that of Voltaire, though he admitted that 'this doctrine, though it might be true, was not very useful' (*A* 59).

Throughout his life, Franklin had much more interest in science than in religion. Already as a child he had invented paddles and flippers to increase his speed of swimming. The 1740s were the period of his greatest scientific endeavour. He discovered the Gulf Stream and conducted studies of the effects of oil on water. He designed new types of stove, invented the damper and attempted to devise a perfect smokeless chimney. But it was in the study of electricity that he made his most lasting contribution to science. He began with experiments on static electricity collected through glass gadgets. Many of the most commonplace words used today in the discussion of electricity – positive, negative, neutral, battery, condenser, conductor – were coined by Franklin in these years. He discovered the fundamental law of the conservation of electric charge, and carried out the experiments that led to the invention of the lightning conductor. His results, published in a pamphlet in 1751 and swiftly translated into French, German and Italian, gave him a European reputation.

Franklin crossed the Atlantic eight times and spent long periods first in London and then in Paris. In 1759 he paid a visit to Scotland, where he met David Hume and Adam Smith and entertained them with his irreverent literary hoaxes. A member of the Pennsylvania Assembly since 1751, he visited England as its agent in a dispute with the descendants of William Penn over their proprietorial rights in Pennsylvania.

While in London in 1765, Franklin met a young English scientist with an interest in electricity, Joseph Priestley

(1733–1804). Encouraged by Franklin, Priestley carried out experiments of his own, which showed that the attraction of electricity, like that of gravity, is as the square of the distances. He went on to publish in 1767 *The History and Present State of Electricity* in a quarter of a million words. He was to go on to have a distinguished career as a chemist, but in his own mind science was little more than a hobby.

The son of a weaver in Leeds, Priestley had been brought up by a Presbyterian aunt, who saw that he received an excellent education in languages at the local grammar school. In 1752 he went to study at a nonconformist academy in Daventry, and three years later became a minister at Needham Market in Suffolk. While studying the Bible there, he ceased to believe in the Trinity and became an Arian. He had to move to a more liberal congregation in Nantwich, where he built a school. He also held a teaching post at the dissenting academy in Warrington, where he transformed the curriculum so that it included English literature, history and science.

In 1767 Priestley started a new ministry at a chapel in Leeds. He ceased to believe that Jesus was in any way divine, and he founded a magazine, *Theological Repository*, to propagate his new Unitarian views. While at Leeds he wrote an *Essay on the First Principles of Government* in which he distinguished between two kinds of liberty: civil and political. The most fundamental was civil liberty, which was freedom from government control over religion and education. Toleration, he argued, must be extended not only to dissenters but to Catholics and atheists. Political liberty – the right to vote and hold office – was something to be decided pragmatically: which groups are most likely to exercise political power for the benefit of the citizens?

From 1773 until 1780, when he moved to Birmingham, Priestley was librarian and adviser to the Whig politician Lord Shelburne. He published several works attacking the radical distinction between soul and body, arguing that dualism resulted from a concept of inert matter that recent science had shown to be untenable. There was no reason to deny that thought could be an operation of a material object like the brain. If human beings were immortal, as Christianity taught, that was only because God, in his good time, would resurrect the human body along with its mental activities.

It was during his time with Shelburne that Priestley made his most significant contribution to chemistry. He had already invented soda water, but it was his 1774 Royal Society paper 'On different kinds of Air' that established his reputation. Traditionally, air had been regarded as an element, and in contemporary science combustion (e.g. of a metal) was explained as the escape into the air of a substance known as phlogiston. An experiment conducted by Priestley in 1774 produced a substance that he called 'dephlogisticated air'. The experiment showed that air was not an element, and the substance that emerged was what we now call oxygen, though Priestley did not accept the theoretical structure implicit in that name. For a further quarter of a century, during which he discovered six hitherto unidentified gases, he continued to believe in the existence of phlogiston.

Benjamin Franklin, at the time when he first met Priestley, had been a great Anglophile and keen royalist. As relations deteriorated between the American colonies and the mother country, more and more of his energy was devoted to preserving the union between them. He found allies in the

British enlightenment community. In 1771 he spent periods with Hume and found him sympathetic. Priestley supported his patron, Shelburne, in seeking to avoid conflict. But the colonists' most energetic supporter was Edmund Burke, who represented New York in London in the same way as Franklin represented Pennsylvania. In the 1760s a succession of Acts of the Westminster Parliament gave offence to the American colonies. The first was the Stamp Act of 1764, which placed a tax on legal transactions. When Burke was elected to Parliament in the following year, his first speeches were eloquent pleas for the repeal of this Act.

After the Act was repealed, the Chancellor of the Exchequer, Charles Townshend, imposed duties on American imports of paint, paper and tea. These too were unpopular, and met with a boycott. Franklin wrote a pamphlet denouncing them. By 1773 only one of these taxes remained – confirmed by a new Tea Act – which was sufficiently unpopular to cause citizens of Boston to board ships in harbour and dump 342 cases of tea into the water.

Burke argued passionately for the repeal of the Tea Act, and as relations across the Atlantic worsened he followed up with a speech of 1775 'On Moving his Resolutions for Conciliations with the Colonies', proclaiming that a nation is not governed that is perpetually to be conquered, and singing the praises of the American love of freedom. The spirit of liberty, he said 'is stronger in the English colonies, probably, than in any other people of the earth'.

To the last minute Franklin held on to the hope that conflict could be avoided. He was shocked by the Boston Tea Party and he held confidential discussions with the elder William Pitt, now Lord Chatham, who led the opposition to the colonial repression policy of the Prime Minister, Lord

North. But by the time Burke had given his great speech, Franklin had given up hope of peacemaking and had already taken ship for Philadelphia.

Once it was clear that war was inevitable, Franklin devoted his scientific expertise to the military activities of the rebels, and his diplomatic skills to the co-ordination of their political efforts. In the latter task he was joined by a Virginian lawyer and parliamentarian named Thomas Jefferson (1743–1826). Jefferson shared the enlightenment enthusiasm for the scientific ideals of Bacon and Newton, and the political ideals of John Locke. He had written pamphlets asserting the rights of the colonists, culminating in a 'Declaration of the Causes and Necessity of Taking up Arms' of 1775. It was to him that the task of drafting the Declaration of Independence was entrusted. Franklin, however, was responsible for some significant changes to the first draft, describing, for instance, the fundamental truths as 'self-evident' rather than 'sacred and undeniable'.

In 1776 Jefferson took a leading part in reforming the laws of Virginia, drafting a statute proclaiming religious freedom. At the same time, Franklin was sent to Paris to negotiate the alliance with France that made possible the American victory in the War of Independence. He renewed his acquaintance with the *philosophes* and was dramatically reunited with Voltaire in 1778 at the Académie Royale just before the latter's death. They shook hands with each other, but the admiring audience insisted they should kiss like Frenchmen, so the two old men gave each other an enormous hug.

Franklin helped to draw up the Treaty of Paris of 1783 that ended the war, and returned to Philadelphia. He was a delegate to the convention of 1787 that framed the US constitution. In the very last year of his life he returned to science and invented bifocal spectacles. He died in 1790 with an arguable claim to be the fullest incarnation of the Enlightenment's scientific and political ideals: he was a better politician than the age's other scientists, and a greater scientist than any of the movement's politicians.

12

Farewell to Hume and Smith

The year 1776 was the climacteric of the Enlightenment. It saw the emergence of a new nation with the American Declaration of Independence, and it saw the consolidation of a new discipline with Adam Smith's *Inquiry into the Nature and Causes of the Wealth of Nations*. It was also the year in which David Hume died and Edward Gibbon began to publish *The History of the Decline and Fall of the Roman Empire*.

Smith's *Inquiry* is a founding document of the science of economics, even though its insistence on the historical, social and moral context of economic activity means that it bears little resemblance to modern mathematical texts of econometrics. It is a substantial work in five books. The first is concerned with the division of labour and the three classes it produces. The second treats of the production and accumulation of wealth. The third is a historical study of the process whereby the feudal economy of the Middle Ages evolved into the capitalism of Smith's own day. The fourth is a critique of two contemporary theories of political economy: mercantilism, which sought to protect domestic economy through high tariffs, and physiocracy, which regarded agriculture as the only source of genuine wealth. The fifth and longest book sets out the scope and limits of government intervention in economic affairs.

The annual product of every country, Smith tells us:

> Divides itself into three parts: the rent of land, the wages of
> labour, and the profits of stock; and constitutes a revenue to
> three different orders of people; to those who live by rent,
> to those who live by wages, and to those who live by profit.
> These are the three great, original and constituent orders of
> every civilized society. (*WN* 155)

In a developed economy, individuals will not only provide
for their own needs but will accumulate a surplus of raw
materials or manufactured goods, which will be available
for trade with others. Manufacturers may find that special-
izing in the production of a single good will enable them, by
trade, to satisfy all their other needs. The division of labour
will enable workers to produce a greater quantity of goods
in a shorter amount of time, until the actual contribution
of an individual labourer to the completed product may be
quite small.

The driving motive of the whole economic system,
according to the *Wealth of Nations*, is the self-interest of the
members of each of the classes:

> Give me that which I want, and you shall have this which
> you want . . . it is in this manner that we obtain from one
> another the far greater part of those good offices which
> we stand in need of. It is not from the benevolence of the
> butcher, the brewer, or the baker, that we expect our dinner,
> but from their regard to their own interest. (*WN* 22)

Every individual continually exerts himself, Smith tells us,
to find the most advantageous employment for whatever
capital he can command. In general, individuals neither
intend to promote the public interest, nor do they know
that they are doing so. Each person directs his industry only

to the maximization of value. '[H]e intends only his own gain, and he is in this, as in many other cases, led by an invisible hand to promote an end which was no part of his intention' (*WN* 292).

In the *Wealth of Nations* we hear no more of the sympathy that had such an important place in *The Theory of Moral Sentiments*, and some critics have seen a complete incompatibility between the two works. But in fact they complement rather than contradict each other. It is surely correct that in our economic transactions – investment, buying, selling, taking profits – self-interest dominates. It is rarely that we buy an item out of pity for the vendor, and it would be eccentric to make a purchase out of compassion for the exchequer. But as Smith well knew, economic activity, however essential, is only a small part of human life.

The invisible hand that takes care of the economy is by itself incompetent to produce human well-being. The last book of the *Wealth of Nations* makes clear that Smith realized that the market, of itself, cannot provide the necessary results. There are, he maintained, three areas where government has the right and the duty to fund and direct the activity of its citizens, namely defence of the realm, the administration of justice, and those pubic works and institutions that are necessary for the community but for which private citizens are unwilling to pay.

Smith was well aware of the demeaning effects of the division of labour in a capitalist economy. Because of the necessary specialization, most labourers perform no more than a few simple repetitive tasks.

> The man whose whole life is spent in performing a few simple operations, of which the effects too are, perhaps,

> always the same, or very nearly the same, has no occasion
> to exert his understanding, or to exercise his invention . . .
> He naturally loses, therefore, the habit of such exertion, and
> generally becomes as stupid and ignorant as it is possible for
> a human creature to become. (*WN* 429)

The remedy for this is that the government should set up, at public expense, a system of compulsory education for the working class in reading, writing, arithmetic and the basics of science.

Shortly after the *Wealth of Nations* was published, David Hume died. To the disappointment of James Boswell (who recorded his final illness in detail), Hume met death serenely, having declined the consolations of religion. He left a brief autobiography, which was brought out a year later by Adam Smith, who wrote of him: 'Upon the whole, I have always considered him, both in his lifetime and since his death, as approaching as nearly to the idea of a perfectly wise and virtuous man, as perhaps the nature of human frailty will admit.'

Hume had spent part of his last years revising a set of *Dialogues Concerning Natural Religion*, a philosophical criticism of natural theology. Smith was unwilling to publish them but they were brought out in 1779 on the authority of Hume's nephew. The dialogues feature three characters: Cleanthes, Philo and Demea. It is not easy to identify which of the three represents Hume himself. Of the three, Demea is the character presented least sympathetically; but both Philo and Cleanthes have been suggested as mouthpieces for their author. It is remarkable that both of them take quite seriously the argument for God's existence from the presence of design in the world.

Cleanthes compares the universe to a great machine divided into an infinite number of smaller machines:

All these various machines, and even their most minute parts,
are adjusted to each other with an accuracy, which ravished
into admiration all men, who have ever contemplated them.
The curious adapting of means to ends, throughout all nature,
resembles exactly, though it much exceeds, the productions
of human contrivance; of human designs, thought, wisdom
and intelligence. Since therefore the effects resemble each
other, we are led to infer, by all the rules of analogy, that
the causes also resemble; and that the Author of Nature is
somewhat similar to the mind of man; though possessed of
much larger faculties, proportioned to the grandeur of the
work, which he has executed.   (*HR* 116)

Philo is critical of this argument but he too, after a detailed
presentation of the problem of evil as a counterbalance, is
willing to say that a Divine Being 'discovers himself to reason in the inexplicable contrivance and artifice of Nature'
(*HR* 189). But his assent to natural theology is very guarded.
He is willing to agree that the cause or causes of order in
the universe probably bear some remote analogy to human
intelligence; but he affirms that this affords no inference
that affects human life or can be the source of any action
or forbearance. The most he is willing to concede is that the
argument from design is of more weight than the objections that lie against it (*HR* 203).

This probably represents Hume's own position. It is clear
that he had not the slightest belief in Christianity, despite
the ironical compliments to it he scatters throughout his
works. But with respect to the existence of God he was an
agnostic, not an atheist. It was not until the triumph of
Darwinism in the next century that an atheist could feel
confident that he had an effective antidote to the argument
from design.

13

Edward Gibbon

Edward Gibbon was born in Putney in 1737, the eldest son of a Kentish horse-racing Tory squire. By the age of ten he had lost his mother and six younger siblings. He was himself a sickly child and his education was erratic; he missed terms during his two years at Westminster School and he picked up what learning he could from precocious reading in his family's libraries. When he went to Magdalen College, Oxford at 15 he was, by his own account, more learned than many a doctor and more ignorant than many a schoolboy.

At Oxford, to the horror of his father, Gibbon turned papist. He was packed off to Lausanne into the care of a Calvinist pastor. Gradually he gave up Catholicism but became a sceptic rather than a convinced Protestant. In later life he looked back to his time there as the foundation of his life as a scholar.

> [I]f my childish revolt against the religion of my country had not stripped me in time of my academic gown, the five important years so liberally improved in the studies and conversation of Lausanne, would have been steeped in port and prejudice among the monks of Oxford. (*A* 85)

During this period he fell in love with Suzanne Curchod, but the marriage was forbidden by his father. 'I sighed as a lover, I obeyed as a son', Gibbon wrote; and Suzanne went on to marry the French financier Jacques Necker and to give birth to the future Madame de Staël.

The most important event of the time in Lausanne was Gibbon's discovery of the writings of Montesquieu. Like all enlightenment thinkers, he was deeply impressed by *The Spirit of the Laws* and the organic view of history it presented, and he wrote in French an essay, dedicated to Suzanne, praising it as a sound guide for a philosophic historian. Montesquieu had also written a lesser-known treatise on the causes of the greatness and decadence of the Romans. It was to be 6 years before Gibbon chose that theme for his own masterpiece, and 14 years before he actually started work on it.

Returning to England at the age of 21, he spent the last two years of the Seven Years War in the Hampshire militia, on guard against a possible French invasion. While on the march he read many a classic text and entertained ideas of several grand projects, including a history of Florence under the Medici and a narrative of the development of the liberties of Switzerland. When the war ended he set off on a grand tour, visiting Paris and returning to Lausanne, still carrying with him a vast classical library. The climax of the tour was a stay in Rome, during which he had a flash of inspiration.

> It was in Rome, on the 15th October 1764, as I sat musing amidst the ruins of the Capitol, while the barefooted friars were singing vespers in the temple of Jupiter, that the idea of writing the decline and fall of the city first started to my mind. (*A* 160)

On his return home he had to devote his attention to his father's illness and death and to restoring the family finances after a generation of mismanagement. What time he had for literary work he devoted to writing the first book of his earlier project, the history of the Swiss. When this was finished he sent it to David Hume, whom he saw as his mentor in historical writing. Hume objected to the fact that it was written in French. The English language, now solidly established in America, Hume foretold, would soon supersede French as the international language.

It was not until 1772 that Gibbon finally settled down to write his Roman history narrative – now not just an account of the fortunes of the city, but of the whole Empire. He finished the first volume within four years, in spite of having become a member of Parliament in 1774 – it helped, perhaps, that he never made a speech there. This first volume took the narrative up to the Emperor Constantine, and concluded with two chapters (XV and XVI) on the early history of Christianity. The book quickly ran through three editions and soon made Gibbon famous. But its success was a *succès de scandale*. Gibbon in a letter wrote that it had been very well received 'except perhaps by the clergy who seem (I know not why) to show their teeth'. He expressed surprise that people took the final chapters as 'nothing less than a satire on the Christian religion'. He should not have been surprised. Hume had already written to him, having read the chapters: 'I think you have observ'd a very prudent Temperament; but it was impossible to treat the subject so as not to give Grounds of Suspicion against you, and you may expect that a Clamour will arise' (*L* 310).

What was it that gave offence? The chapters in question set out to describe by what means the Christian faith obtained its remarkable victory over the established religions of the Roman Empire. They offer five causes for the rapid growth of the Church:

1 The intolerant zeal of the Christians, inherited from the Jews.
2 The doctrine of a future life.
3 The miraculous powers ascribed to the primitive Church.
4 The pure and austere morals of the Christians.
5 The discipline of the Christian community, gradually growing into an independent state in the heart of the Empire.

It was found offensive that none of these causes included the providential guidance of the Holy Spirit. Critics were not pacified by Gibbon's initial statement that he was looking only for the secondary causes, and not the primary cause, of the growth of Christianity. Again, the treatment of miracles was regarded as incompatible with orthodoxy. In fact more circumspect than Hume, Gibbon did not deny that miracles might offer a vindication of religious claims, and he did not deny that the miracles recorded in the Gospels might actually have occurred. He merely explained why the credulous environment of the early Christian centuries may have made it easy for converts to accept the Gospel narratives. The nearest he goes to denying the Christian miracles is the following:

> Since every friend to revelation is persuaded of the reality, and every reasonable man is convinced of the cessation, of miraculous powers, it is evident that there must have been *some period* in which they were either suddenly or gradually withdrawn from the Christian church. Whatever era is chosen for that purpose, the death of the apostles, the conversion of the Roman Empire, or the extinction of

the Arian heresy, the insensibility of the Christians who
lived at that time will equally afford a just matter of surprise.
(*DF* II.115)

In fact it was the tone as much as the content of Gibbon's
writing that gave offence to the godly. Certainly, among the
great enlightenment writers, he was the consummate master
of irony – more polite than Voltaire, more deadly than Hume.
He could rightly claim never to have written a sentence dis-
paraging of Jesus – but he could not resist the occasional
footnote such as this about a Cappadocian wonderworker:

Apollonius of Tyana was born about the same time as Jesus
Christ. His life (that of the former) is related in so fabulous
a manner by his disciples, that we are at a loss to discover
whether he was a sage, an impostor, or a fanatic.

The insertion of the parenthesis is masterly – but this
kind of thing justifies the complaint of James Boswell that
Gibbon 'should have warned us of our danger, before we
entered his garden of flowery eloquence, by advertising
"spring guns and man-traps set here"'.

It is hard to take seriously Gibbon's surprise at the clerical
reaction to his volume. He remained silent in reply, until he
was accused not only of infidelity but of scholarly inaccur-
acy and dishonesty. He responded with a *Vindication* that
has been, ever since, regarded as an overwhelming victory
over his critics. He decided to continue the history through
the period of the Byzantine Empire up to the Renaissance.
Two volumes appeared in 1781, a fourth in 1783 and a final
three were published in 1788, concluding with a magnifi-
cent account of the fall of Constantinople in 1453.

During the American Revolution, Gibbon took the opposite side from his enlightenment colleagues, becoming

a member of Lord North's government. When North fell in 1782, he moved to Lausanne, where he wrote the final volumes of his history. In the meantime he had spent a few months in Paris with the Neckers, conversing with Diderot and d'Alembert. He had lost his youthful admiration for Voltaire, whom he now considered 'a bigot, an intolerant bigot', who 'insulted the religion of nations'. Moreover he criticized 'the Gallic frenzy, the wild theories of equal and boundless freedom'. He lived on until 1794, a witness of the excesses of that frenzy.

14

Jeremy Bentham

The year 1789 was remarkable in the history of both politics and literature, just as 1776 had been. The outbreak of the French Revolution coincided with the publication of the Enlightenment's most significant contribution to ethics, Jeremy Bentham's *An Introduction to the Principles of Morals and Legislation*. This book became the founding charter of the school of thought known as Utilitarianism.

Bentham was born in 1748, the son of a prosperous London attorney. A precocious child, he was sent to Westminster School at the age of 7 and entered university when 12. All the young geniuses who were sent to Oxford in the eighteenth century found their education there unsatisfactory: Adam Smith at Balliol, Gibbon at Magdalen and now Bentham at the Queen's College. Bentham was particularly repelled by the law lectures of the famous jurist William Blackstone.

Destined for a legal career, he was called to the Bar when 21, but never practised. Instead he devoted himself to legal theory. The cumbrous and incoherent English legal system, he believed, needed to be reconstructed on the basis of sound principles of jurisprudence. The most important such principle was that of utility: the real standard of morality and the true goal of legislation was the greatest happiness of the greatest number.

During the 1770s Bentham wrote a dissertation on the purpose and limits of punishment, drawing on the *Dei delitti e delle pene* of the great Italian jurist Cesare Beccaria (1738–94), who had attacked judicial torture and capital punishment. During the same period, Bentham worked on a critique of Blackstone's *Commentaries on the Laws of England*. A portion of this was published in 1776 as *A Fragment on Government*, which begins with an enlightenment manifesto:

> The age we live in is a busy age; in which knowledge is rapidly advancing towards perfection. In the natural world, in particular, every thing teems with discovery and with improvement . . . Corresponding to discovery and improvement in the natural world is reformation in the moral: if that which seems a common notion be, indeed, a true one, that in the moral world there no longer remains any matter for discovery. Perhaps, however, this may not be the case . . . with so little method and precision have the consequences of this fundamental axiom, *it is the greatest happiness of the greatest number that is the measure of right and wrong*, been as yet developed.
>
> (*FG* vi; Bentham's emphasis)

The book goes on to demolish the notion of a social contract and to ridicule Blackstone's panegyric on the British constitution as the best of all possible governments.

The *Fragment on Government* attracted the attention of the Earl of Shelburne, Priestley's patron, who was later briefly Prime Minister. Bentham was introduced by Shelburne to political circles in England and France. Among his new English friends was a niece of Charles James Fox, Caroline Fox, to whom he made an unsuccessful proposal of marriage in 1805. Most important of the French acquaintances was Étienne Dumont, tutor to Shelburne's son, who was later to publish a number of Bentham's works in translation. For a while Bentham was better known in France than in Britain.

Like Diderot, Bentham travelled to Russia to offer constitutional advice to Catherine the Great. In the course of travels between 1785 and 1787, he stayed with his brother Samuel on the estate of Prince Potemkin, where he conceived the idea of a novel kind of prison, the panopticon. This was a circular building with a central observation point from which the jailer could keep a permanent eye on the inmates. He returned from Russia full of enthusiasm for prison reform, and tried to persuade both the British and French governments to erect a model prison on his plan. He failed in each case, but the French Assembly made him an honorary citizen and the British Parliament eventually voted him the giant sum of £23,000 in compensation for his work on the scheme.

The publication of the *Introduction* in 1789 set out in full a moral system based on the greatest happiness principle. Unlike previous philosophers, Bentham identified happiness with pleasure: it is pleasure that is the supreme spring of action. The *Introduction* famously begins:

> Nature has placed mankind under the governance of two sovereign masters, pain and pleasure. It is for them alone to point out what we ought to do, as well as to determine what we shall do. On the one hand, the standard of right and wrong, on the other the chain of causes and effects, are fastened to their throne. They govern us in all we do, in all we say, in all we think: every effort we can make to throw off our subjection, will serve but to demonstrate and confirm it. (*P* 1.1)

To maximize happiness, therefore, for Bentham, was the same thing as to maximize pleasure.

Bentham's hedonism was not a call to sensuality: he was careful to point out that pleasure was a sensation that could be caused not only by eating and drinking and sex, but also by a multitude of other things, as varied as the acquisition of wealth, kindness to animals or belief in the favour of a Supreme Being. The value of each and every pleasure, he maintained, was the same, no matter how it was caused. 'Quantity of pleasure being equal', he wrote, 'push-pin is as good a poetry.' What went for pleasure went for pain too: the quantity of pain, and not its cause, is the measure of its disvalue.

The quantification of pleasure and pain, therefore, is of prime importance, and it is no trivial task. Bentham offers recipes for their measurement. Pleasure A counts more than pleasure B if it is more intense, or if it lasts longer, or if it is more certain, or if it is more immediate. In the 'felicific calculus' of our own affairs these different factors must be taken into account and weighed against each other. If we are looking beyond our own affairs, we must further consider another factor, which Bentham calls 'extension'; that is, how widely the pains and pleasures will be spread across the population. When we are determining public policy, extension is the crucial factor.

Bentham commended utilitarianism by contrasting it with other ethical systems. The second chapter of the *Introduction* is entitled 'Of Principles adverse to that of Utility'. He lists two such principles, the first being that of asceticism and the second that of sympathy and antipathy. The principle of asceticism is the policy of pursuing the greatest misery of the greatest number: such a principle, Bentham admits, 'never was, nor ever can be, consistently pursued by any living creature' (*P* 2.10). Someone who accepts the principle of sympathy and antipathy, on the other hand, judges actions as good or bad to the extent that they accord or not with his own feelings (*P* 2.2).

The principle of sympathy and antipathy is a catch-all that includes moral systems of very different kinds, including those proposed by enlightenment thinkers such as Hume and Adam Smith. Sympathy and antipathy, Bentham says, may be given various fancy names: moral sense, common sense, understanding, rule of right, fitness of things, law of nature, right reason and so on. Moral systems that present themselves under such banners, Bentham believes, are all simply placing a grandiose screen in front of an appeal to individual subjective feeling. 'They consist all of them in so many contrivances for avoiding the obligation of appealing to any external standard, and for prevailing upon the reader to accept of the author's sentiment or opinion as a reason for itself' (*P* 2.14).

In 1808 Bentham became friends with a Scottish philosopher, James Mill, who persuaded him to focus on political and constitutional reform rather than criticisms of legal procedure and practice. Three years on, Bentham proposed to US President James Madison that he should draw up a constitutional code for the United States, and in his later years had hopes that his constitutional code would be implemented in Latin America by Simón Bolívar, the President of Colombia.

In 1817 Bentham published a *Catechism of Parliamentary Reform* and followed it up with the draft of a radical reform bill. He started to compose, but never completed, a constitutional code for the UK. By the end of his life he had become convinced that the existing British constitution was a screen hiding a conspiracy of the rich against the poor. He therefore advocated the abolition of the monarchy and the House of Lords, the introduction of annual parliaments elected by universal suffrage, and the disestablishment of the Church of England.

With a group of like-minded radicals, whose organ was the *Westminster Review*, Bentham helped to establish University College London, which opened its doors in 1828. This was the first University-level institution in Britain to admit students without religious tests. There, in accordance with his will, Bentham's remains were placed after his death, and there, clothed and topped with a wax head, they survive to this day – his 'auto-icon' as he termed it. A more appropriate memorial to his endeavours was the Great Reform Bill, widely extending the parliamentary franchise, which passed into law a few weeks before he died in 1832.

15

The French Revolution

It was a Frenchman who first saw the significance of Priestley's experiments on gases, described in Chapter 11: Antoine-Laurent Lavoisier (1743–94). A Parisian lawyer and later tax-collector, he first made his mark in science when in 1766 he was awarded a medal by the Académie Royale for an essay on street lighting. In 1772 he proved by experiment that when sulphur burns it gains weight, rather than losing it, as the phlogiston theory demanded. Learning of Priestley's work, he carried out similar experiments on his own, producing samples of 'pure air'. He showed that combustion could take place only in the presence of such a gas, and that in the course of combustion it was absorbed, adding weight to the body in question. He named the gas 'oxygen' as part of a new nomenclature of elements (including 'hydrogen' and 'sulphuric acid'), which greatly facilitated the progress of chemistry.

Lavoisier also showed that respiration in humans and animals is a form of combustion. We keep up our body heat by combining the carbon in our food with the oxygen we inhale, and thus produce the carbon dioxide that we breathe out. Another fundamental discovery of Lavoisier was that water was a compound of hydrogen and oxygen. The system inherited from the Greeks, of the four elements of earth, air, fire and water, was at last permanently displaced in favour of a new table of elements, of which

Lavoisier laid the foundations. His work was summed up in an *Elements of Chemistry* that was published in 1789, the year of the French Revolution.

A colleague of Lavoisier elected to the French Academy in 1782 was a young mathematician, the Marquis de Condorcet, a protégé of d'Alembert who had contributed to the *Encyclopédie*. He won fame for an essay on the integral calculus, but his speciality was the analysis of probabilities. This branch of mathematics, he believed, would enable the social sciences to approximate to the certainty of the physical sciences. He argued this in an essay of 1785, 'On the Application of Analysis to the Probability of majority Opinions', in which he presented the rudiments of what he called 'social arithmetic'. In the last years of the *ancien régime* he and his wife, Sophie de Grouchy, maintained a salon conspicuous for its support for toleration, reform and the abolition of slavery.

Condorcet was the only senior *philosophe* to play an active part in the French Revolution. As a member of the Paris municipal council he attended its early debates and became a member of the Legislative Assembly in 1791, becoming in 1792 its President. He devoted much effort to the drafting of a republican constitution and to the elaboration of a system of public education. But his opposition to the execution of the King and Queen led to his exclusion from government and exile from Paris.

In the *Sketch for a Historical Tableau of the Progress of the Human Mind*, his last work, left incomplete, Condorcet argued for a perfect equality of rights between the sexes, and traced the history of human progress through nine epochs, from a state of nature prior to society up to the societies of modern Europe. He looked forward to a tenth epoch in which, freed from ignorance, bigotry and tyranny, humanity would continue in a perpetual path of progress. To assist this progress, he advocated a universal scientific language and a decimal system of classification.

In these early days several enlightenment figures abroad saw the developments in France as an embodiment of their ideals. After all, during its early years the revolutionary government enacted many measures that had long been advocated by the *philosophes*: for instance, the abolition of ranks and titles, the closure of the slave trade, the opening of public office to all including Protestants, Jews and atheists. In England, Joseph Priestley was as enthusiastic about the French Revolution as he had been about the American one. When the 'Friends of the Revolution' held a dinner in Birmingham to commemorate the fall of the Bastille, Priestley's house was burned down by a mob, though he had not himself been present at the dinner.

In 1789 Edmund Burke had written: 'The spirit it is impossible not to admire.' However, his enthusiasm for the revolution was from the outset highly qualified, and it did not survive the imprisonment of Louis XVI and Marie Antoinette, which provoked him to his best-known and most anti-Enlightenment utterance: 'The age of chivalry is gone. That of sophisters, economists and calculators has succeeded, and the glory of Europe is extinguished for ever.' His eloquent, voluminous, witty and waspish *Reflections on the Revolution in France* (1790) took the form of a letter to a friend in Paris in which he denounced the doctrine of natural rights proclaimed by the French National Assembly in August 1789. It was quite wrong, he affirmed, to say that a king owed his crown to the choice of his people. It was preposterous to claim that the people are entitled to choose their own governors, cashier them for misconduct and frame a form of government to their liking.

The notion of such individual political rights, according to Burke, ignored the role of history and society in the establishment of constitutions. The stock of reason in private persons is small: 'individuals would do better to avail themselves of the general bank and capital of nations, and of ages'. Society is a partnership not only of those now living but also of generations past and generations yet unborn.

The liberty of which the French boasted had not, Burke claimed, produced a just and effective government. Instead it had proved irreconcilable with the discipline of armies, with the collection of fair and adequate revenue and with the solidity of property. It had led to a breakdown of peace and order and of civil and social manners. What Burke was most afraid of was that the principles of the revolution might take root in England. He ended by saying: 'I wish my countrymen rather to recommend to our neighbours the example of the British constitution than to take models from them for the improvement of our own. In the former they have got an invaluable treasure' (*RRF* 375).

Joseph Priestley wrote a response to Burke's *Reflections* in 1791, following it up with a political dialogue in which he argued for republican reform of the House of Commons. He was offered a seat in the French National Assembly, but in 1794, the year in which Condorcet died in prison and Lavoisier was guillotined, he emigrated to America, settling in Northumberland, Pennsylvania, where he continued to maintain his Unitarian beliefs. He corresponded with Thomas Jefferson about religion until his death in 1804.

16

The rights of men and women

The member of the Enlightenment who continued longest to defend the ideals and support the conduct of revolutionary France was the American Thomas Paine. In 1791 and 1792 he published in two parts a treatise with the title *Rights of Man: Being an Answer to Mr Burke's Attack on the French Revolution. Rights of Man* can claim to be the last great text of the Enlightenment, just as *The Spirit of the Laws* was its first. Paine and Montesquieu address some of the same topics, but from very different angles. Whereas Montesquieu saw the British constitution as a model of the separation of powers, Paine thought it lacked any effective checks or balances. In its place he held up for admiration the declaration of human rights of the French National Assembly of 1789, which Burke had mocked.

The French Revolution was not the first revolution Paine had supported and defended. Born in Norfolk in 1737, and initially a Quaker, he had emigrated to Philadelphia in 1774 with a letter of recommendation from Benjamin Franklin. In January 1776 he published, anonymously, a pamphlet of 47 pages entitled *Common Sense*, which was believed by many of the 120,000 people who bought copies of it to have been written by Franklin himself. The tract argued strongly against hereditary rule: there was no good reason for the distinction of men into kings and subjects. 'Of more worth is one honest man to society and in the sight of God, than all the crowned ruffians that ever lived.'

The pamphlet did much to encourage the revolutionary forces, and when they seemed to waver a year later he followed it up with a call for steadfastness:

> These are the times that try men's souls. The summer soldier and the sunshine patriot will, in this crisis, shrink from the service of their country; but he that stands it now, deserves the love and thanks of every man and woman.

After the war Paine became clerk to the Pennsylvania assembly but devoted much of his time to planning the construction of a single-arched iron bridge over the Schuylkill River. Frustrated by bureaucratic delays, he migrated overseas in 1787 in the hope of selling his concept in France. By now Thomas Jefferson had succeeded Franklin as the US ambassador in Paris, and he befriended Paine, who became useful to the leaders of the revolution and was in 1792 elected to the National Convention.

Shortly earlier the remains of Voltaire and Rousseau had been removed to the Panthéon, the mausoleum that revolutionary France consecrated to the great men of the nation. Enemies in life, the two now lie side by side in the crypt, but neither in death nor in life can their ideals be reconciled. Voltaire would have been horrified by the intolerance and cruelty that disfigured successive revolutionary governments, while many people, then and now, place the responsibility for those excesses at Rousseau's door. Paine wrote that the writings of Rousseau breathed a loveliness of sentiment in favour of liberty; of Voltaire he said that he merited the thanks, rather than the esteem, of humankind.

Rights of Man defended the French Bill of Rights, which commenced as follows:

I   I Men are born, and always continue, free and equal in respect of their rights. Civil distinctions, therefore, can be founded only on public utility.
II The end of all political associations is the preservation of the natural and imprescriptible rights of man; and these rights are liberty, property, security, and resistance of oppression.
III The nation is essentially the source of all sovereignty, nor can any individual or body of men be entitled to any authority which is not expressly derived from it.
(*RM* 162)

Paine argued that the remaining 14 articles of the convention – about such matters as freedom from arbitrary arrest, the presumption of innocence, freedom of speech – followed from these first three. He went on to argue from these premises that democracy is superior to aristocracy, and that leadership should depend on talent and experience rather than heredity.

On the theoretical questions at issue between Burke and Paine, there is no doubt that Paine had the better of the argument. But Burke turned out to be much the better prophet. As the revolution progressed it violated many of the principles enunciated in its statement of human rights. Paine opposed the execution of Louis XVI and Marie Antoinette, and in consequence was imprisoned by Robespierre. He narrowly escaped execution, being released only at the insistence of James Monroe, who had succeeded Jefferson as ambassador. He returned to the USA in 1802 and remained there until his death in 1809.

At the height of the reign of terror, Robespierre could claim that he was expressing Rousseau's general will, and forcing the citizens to be free. Who was in a position to contradict him? Thomas Carlyle, author of *The French Revolution*, was once reproached by a businessman for being too interested in mere ideas: 'There was once a man called Rousseau', Carlyle replied, 'who wrote a book containing nothing but ideas. The second edition was bound in the skins of those who laughed at the first.'

Jefferson, having returned to the USA, became George Washington's first Secretary of State. He was an advocate of states' rights and an opponent of the federalist party of Alexander Hamilton. Though Vice-President under John Adams, Jefferson took little part in government until he was himself chosen as President by the House of Representatives in 1801. In theory a stern opponent of slavery, on which he had written an outspoken tract in 1781, he was never, because of his chronic indebtedness, able to afford to emancipate his own slaves. However, during his term in office the USA went to war with Tripoli to subdue the slave-trading Barbary pirates in the Mediterranean, and one of the last acts of his presidency was the prohibition of the import of slaves.

In Europe, for a while the rise of Napoleon Bonaparte gave renewed grounds for hope that enlightenment values might take root on French soil. The young Bonaparte was an avid reader of Voltaire and Rousseau, and sceptical of religion; several of his early political actions sought to establish institutions of which the *philosophes* would have approved. In a whirlwind visit to Malta in 1798, for instance, he dismantled the clerical government of the Knights of St John, framed a new constitution, abolished slavery, gave permission for the building of a synagogue and added a science

department to the university. Later he made an uninten-
tional contribution to the perpetuation of enlightenment
ideas when, during a financial crisis, he sold the territory of
Louisiana to President Jefferson, thereby doubling the area
of the USA.

In 1809 Jefferson retired to Monticello, his estate in
Virginia. A talented amateur architect, he spent his last
years on the construction of his mansion and the invention
of ingenious, if commonly impractical, domestic devices.
He also devoted time to the improvement of farming and to
the study of palaeontology. The major achievement of his
retirement was the foundation of the University of Virginia.
Until his death in 1826 he kept alight in Virginia the ideals
of the Enlightenment.

Long before then, they had been snuffed out in Europe
as the power of Napoleon became more and more absolute. Among those who admired the young Bonaparte was
Ludwig van Beethoven. When in 1802 Napoleon was proclaimed First Consul for life, and there was a temporary peace
between France and Austria, the 32-year-old composer considered moving to Paris and shortly after began to compose
his third symphony, which he entitled *Bonaparte*. The score
was finished by April 1804, but a month later Beethoven
learned that Napoleon had been declared Emperor. 'So he
too', he exclaimed, 'is nothing more than an ordinary man!
Now he will trample all human rights underfoot and only
pander to his own ambition.' He tore the title page of the
symphony in two and threw it on the floor. When it was
published in 1806 it bore the title 'Heroic symphony, composed to celebrate the memory of a great man'.

The European powers that formed coalitions to resist and
eventually dethrone the Emperor Napoleon were no more

sympathetic than he had become to the Enlightenment. Of the war effort of the English people, G. K. Chesterton wrote memorably:

> In foam and fame at Trafalgar, and on Albuera's plains
> They fought and died like lions, to keep themselves
> in chains.

A few individuals in England continued to press for reform according to enlightenment ideals, and indeed to carry them to unprecedented extremes. Mary Wollstonecraft (1759–97), in her *Vindication of the Rights of Woman* (1792), argued that virtue was neutral between the sexes, and consisted in the development of natural faculties common to both men and women. The conventional allocation of different roles to the different sexes was as artificial and corrupt as the conventional distinctions of rank and power. Political structures should be reformed to take account of this novel conception of private virtue.

In 1797 Wollstonecraft married William Godwin (1756–1836), whose early career had resembled that of Joseph Priestley. Having been for five years a dissenting minister, he lost his faith and after a period as a hack novelist published a radical *Enquiry Concerning Political Justice* (1793). This rejected all of Montesquieu's three types of society – monarchy, aristocracy and democracy – in favour of absolute anarchy. A criminal should not be punished for his actions, because in committing his crime he was no more free than the weapons he used. In the ideal society, citizens co-operate without compulsion.

Institutions such as marriage, the family and legal contracts, Godwin believed, could not oblige us to act otherwise than was required by the intention to promote general happiness. If one's mother was the chambermaid to a learned scholar and both were in a burning building, it was the scholar one should rescue, if only one of the two could be saved. Like Bentham, Godwin denied that there were natural rights, but he made an exception for the right of private judgement.

It is remarkable that in the age of counter-revolution, Godwin escaped prosecution for his writings and survived for many years. After one brilliant novel – *The Adventures of Caleb Williams* – he went back to hack writing to support himself. His marriage to Wollstonecraft lasted less than a year. Mary died in 1797 in giving birth to a daughter who, when she married the poet Percy Shelley, provided a link between the age of the Enlightenment and the Romantic period.

If one were to choose an arbitrary terminus for the Enlightenment as a movement, in the way we chose the Battle of Culloden to mark its beginning, the most appropriate date would be 2 December 1804. On that day Napoleon crowned himself with a replica of Charlemagne's crown in the Cathedral of Notre Dame, in the presence of Pope Pius VII, with whom he had signed a concordat two years previously. *Écrasez l'infâme* had given way to *Embrasez l'infâme*.

Part 2

THE LEGACY

17

The cultural legacy

It can be argued that the Enlightenment was devoured by its own children. The empiricist theory of knowledge that underpinned its faith in scientific progress was shown to be untenable by the great German philosopher Immanuel Kant (1724–1804). The belief that the progress of science would lead inevitably to the betterment of human nature was attacked in theory by Jean-Jacque Rousseau and discredited in practice by the excesses of his Jacobin followers. Napoleon, who in his younger days had set up enlightened structures of government in the countries he occupied, eventually killed off the Enlightenment and gave it church burial.

After 1815, Napoleon's victorious enemies did their best to challenge the ideals and reverse the successes of the Enlightenment. The Waterloo Chamber in Windsor Castle displays the portraits of the absolute monarchs who at the Congress of Vienna had retained or regained their thrones, and of the Pope and Cardinal who were allowed to share in dictating the structure of a reactionary Europe. In many countries the clergy regained much of the power they had lost during the revolutionary era, and as the century progressed there were revivals of conservative religion. A typical example was the Oxford Movement, which sought to remodel the Church of England to bring it into line with its medieval and Catholic past. The Vatican Council of 1870, which declared that the Pope was the infallible primate of all Christianity, exalted papal claims to their highest point since the thirteenth-century pontificate of Boniface VIII. Only in the United States did the candle lit in the 1770s continue to shine undimmed.

In literature the Romantic movement swept away the ethos of the eighteenth century. In France Voltaire had in his lifetime been renowned as a poet, and in Germany Schiller's 'Ode to Joy' had been seen by many as an international anthem of the Enlightenment. But in England the Enlightenment had not produced great poetry: the two most significant poets of the latter part of the eighteenth century, Christopher Smart and William Blake, were both in different ways hostile to the movement. By the 1820s even William Wordsworth (who during the French Revolution had counted it bliss to be alive and heaven to be young) and Samuel Taylor Coleridge (who with him had nearly been arrested as a revolutionary spy) had settled down as conservative supporters of traditional and ecclesiastical institutions. The philosopher John Stuart Mill tells us that it was only by pairing the teaching of the utilitarian Bentham with that of the Romantic Coleridge that he was able to achieve a balanced view of human nature.

Unlike the Renaissance, which encompassed all branches of culture simultaneously, the Enlightenment did not directly affect music, painting and architecture. To be sure, there are great musical masterpieces that embody enlightenment ideals: Mozart's *Magic Flute* and Beethoven's *Fidelio* spring to mind. But in these operas it is through the plot and the libretto, not the music as such, that the Enlightenment finds expression. Though orchestral music became available to a wide public in the eighteenth century, there is no enlightenment novelty in musical technique parallel to the change from plainsong to polyphony. Similarly with painting: there is no enlightenment innovation to parallel the development of perspective and chiaroscuro in the centuries of the Renaissance.

The counter-Enlightenment, however, was reflected in the visual arts. The Pre-Raphaelite movement in Britain was a deliberate return to the values of a period that preceded not only the Enlightenment but also the Renaissance. Throughout Europe, Gothic architecture came into fashion in municipal as well as ecclesiastical building. Even in domestic architecture, the Victorian period showed a preference for shade and gloom rather than the ample and airy lighting of the eighteenth century.

What was common to all these nineteenth-century developments was an ambivalence about the notion of progress. Prior to the Enlightenment, people looking for ideals had looked backwards in time, whether to the primitive Church, classical antiquity or to some mythical prelapsarian era. It was a key doctrine of the Enlightenment that the human race, so far from falling from some earlier eminence, was moving forwards to a happier future, to be made possible by the development of the natural and social sciences.

The sciences did, of course, take massive strides forwards in the nineteenth century, and the benefits they made possible were celebrated by such events as the Great Exhibition of 1851. But the most fundamental of the century's scientific discoveries, that of evolution by natural selection, was initially not a forward-looking but a backward-looking discovery. For many years it fell outside the enlightenment category of 'useful knowledge': it was of more interest to history, archaeology and theology than to medicine or biology.

It was only much later, when Darwinian theory was combined with Mendelian genetics, that the way was open for improvements in agriculture and medicine through genetic modification.

During the nineteenth century the most visible effects of scientific advances were the Industrial Revolution and the improvement of communication. Initially the Industrial Revolution exhibited more of the negative effects of the division of labour that Adam Smith had regretted than the positive ones he extolled. The improvement of communication, paradoxically, had significant reactionary effects. The ease of travel spurred the missionary efforts of many Christian denominations, spreading a gospel quite different from the enlightenment messages of plurality and toleration. The efficiency of communication meant that Pope Pius IX had much greater control over his bishops throughout the world than any eighteenth-century pope had over the French prelates Voltaire ridiculed.

As in religion, so in politics: improved travel and communication facilitated not democracy but imperialism. To be sure, within Europe most countries over the century saw modest extensions of the franchise, but even there, in countries like Italy and Germany, these improvements were accompanied with triumphal nationalism. Elsewhere, large tracts of the world were incorporated into empires subjugated to European nation states.

It might be thought that the rise of Marxism was a continuation of the materialism of d'Holbach and his colleagues. It is true that Marxists shared with those philosophers a disbelief in, and hostility to, any notion of an afterlife. But Marxist materialism was unlike the scientific investigation of the human machine that fascinated enlightenment inquirers. It was a dialectical materialism whose guiding principles were derived not from empirical inquiry but from the metaphysical categories of the successors of Kant. And when in the course of time Marxist principles were enshrined in the governments of states, their actual implementation was at the opposite pole from the Enlightenment's emphasis on human rights.

The horrific wars between nation states during the first half of the twentieth century showed how sadly deluded were the hopes of Tom Paine when in 1791 he predicted that within seven years, monarchy and aristocracy would be abolished in Europe, wars would cease and armies and navies could be disbanded. But when peace finally came in 1945 the world took breath, and surveying the wreckage that the counter-Enlightenment had brought, it nerved itself to return to enlightenment values. Since the foundation of the United Nations, and its Universal Declaration of Human Rights, many enlightenment precepts have been observed in the West and have received lip service throughout the world. In the remaining chapters I will explore the current legacy of the Enlightenment in the three areas of religion, morality and politics.

18

The religious legacy

One of the great causes upheld by enlightenment thinkers was the need for religious toleration. However, as the Enlightenment was in its final days, Tom Paine argued that toleration was not enough – what was needed was complete liberty of conscience: 'Toleration is not the opposite of Intolerance, but is the counterfeit of it. The one assumes to itself the right of with-holding liberty of conscience, and the other of granting it' (*RM* 137).

In support of the case for universal liberty of conscience, Paine imagines a large family of children who are celebrating their father's birthday, each of them offering him a different kind of present:

> Some would pay their congratulations in themes of verse or prose, by some little devices, as their genius dictated, or according to what they thought would please; and perhaps, the least of all, not able to do any of those things, would ramble into the garden, or the field, and gather what it thought the prettiest flower it could find, though, perhaps, it might be but a simple weed. The parent would be more gratified by such variety, than if the whole of them had acted on a concerted plan, and each had made exactly the same offering. (*RM* 324)

The thing that would most distress the parent would be to learn that after the party they had all got together by the ears, boys and girls fighting, scratching and abusing each other about which present was the best one. 'Why may we not suppose, that the great Father of all is pleased with variety of devotion; and that the greatest offence we can act, is that by which we seek to torment and render each other miserable?' (*RM* 324).

With regard to religious freedom, how does the situation today compare with that at the time of the Enlightenment? The United Nations Universal Declaration of Human Rights on this issue sides with Paine rather than with Voltaire. The right that it proclaims to freedom of conscience and religion is expressly said to include the right to the public practice of religion and the right to change one's religion.

The Second Vatican Council of the Roman Catholic Church also declared that the human person has a right to religious freedom:

> This freedom means that all men are to be immune from coercion on the part of individuals or of social groups and of any human power, in such wise that no one is to be forced to act in a manner contrary to his own beliefs, whether privately or publicly, whether alone or in association with others, within due limits.
>
> (*Declaration on Religious Freedom*, para. 2)

The religious freedom defended by the Council has more in common with the toleration commended by Voltaire than with Paine's idea of the equal rights of all religions. The Council reaffirms that there is just one true faith, and its principal concern is the protection of the adherents of that faith from interference by civil government in its practice. However, it does state that immunity from coercion must extend to those who are in religious error. In introducing religious practices, it states, everyone ought at all times to refrain from any manner of action that might seem to carry a hint of coercion, and no one is to be forced to embrace the Christian faith against his or her own will.

One may wonder how far the Vatican declaration is derived from specifically Christian teaching and how far it is consistent with the history of the Church. The declaration admits that the Christian revelation does not affirm in so many words the right of humans to immunity from external coercion in matters religious. The nearest it comes to an apology for past persecutions by the Church is as follows:

> In the life of the People of God, as it has made its pilgrim way through the vicissitudes of human history, there has at times appeared a way of acting that was hardly in accord with the spirit of the Gospel or even opposed to it. Nevertheless, the doctrine of the Church that no one is to be coerced into faith has always stood firm.
>
> (*Declaration on Religious Freedom*, para. 12)

Historically, however, the point at which persecution operated was not at entry to the Church but at departure from it. It was not when you refused to become a Catholic that you risked burning, but when you wished to cease being one and to adopt beliefs and practices the Church judged as heretical.

At the present time there does not seem to be any Christian nation or denomination that seeks to enforce religious orthodoxy by physical coercion. Threats to religious freedom come from other faiths. While most Muslim countries tolerate the practice of other religions, there are countries where apostasy from Islam is punishable by death, and in recent years Islam has spawned a variety of militant sects. Even Buddhists, whose tranquil and peaceable religion was much admired by Voltaire, have in places shown themselves capable of ferocious violence.

So far as concerns the relationship between different religious groups it would be hard to claim that the present age has achieved the goals set out by the thinkers of the Enlightenment. But internally, within mainstream Christian churches, the influence of the Enlightenment is very strong. This is most easily illustrated in the case of the study and interpretation of the Bible.

Enlightenment thinkers such as Voltaire, Reimarus and Lessing – following a tradition going back as far as the great Jewish philosopher Spinoza – subjected the Bible to radical criticism, pointing out the inconsistencies, historical errors and fictions it contained. In particular they stressed that the Pentateuch could not possibly have been written by Moses, that there is no doctrine of immortality in the Old Testament, and that the New Testament accounts of the Resurrection contradict each other.

While, in the nineteenth century, most Christians still treated the Bible as an inspired and infallible text, the critical examination of its content was continued and extended by scholars in several countries. In Germany and France criticism was taken to sceptical extremes. David Strauss, in a life of Jesus translated into English by George Eliot in 1846, endeavoured to show that the Gospel narratives were a succession of myths. He was followed by Ernest Renan, whose sceptical but romantic *Life of Jesus* became a bestseller when it was published in 1863.

British theologians were more cautious than their continental colleagues. Several of them in 1860 brought out a collection entitled *Essays and Reviews* in which the Platonic scholar Benjamin Jowett argued that the Bible must be treated just like any other book. This brought him before the Vice-Chancellor's Court in Oxford, and his fellow essayist, Frederick Temple, had to disown the *Essays* before going on to become Archbishop of Canterbury in 1897. After the turn of the century, however, Anglican divines began to accept many of the conclusions of continental higher criticism.

Slowest to accept the critical study of the Bible was the Roman Catholic Church. In the first decade of the twentieth century, Pope Pius X employed the Pontifical Biblical Commission, set up in 1902, to review opinions put forward by Scripture scholars. A series of decisions from 1905 to 1910 affirmed the substantial Mosaic authorship of the Pentateuch, and the literal historical nature of the first three chapters of Genesis. With regard to the New Testament, the commission affirmed the historicity of the narratives of Jesus' infancy and insisted on an early date for the composition of the Gospels. It rejected specifically the idea that Matthew's Gospel was written after the fall of Jerusalem.

It was not until Pius XII's encyclical *Divino Afflante Spiritu* of 1943 that the Vatican recognized the variety of literary genres in the Bible. This was followed by a letter to the Archbishop of Paris recognizing that the early chapters of Genesis were not 'history in the classical or modern sense'. Since the Second Vatican Council the attitude of Catholic exegetes has become greatly relaxed, with theologians in good standing treating the infancy narratives as beautiful and instructive legends. Dom Henry Wansbrough, a biblical scholar widely respected internationally and himself a member of the Biblical Commission, has defended the view that the debates between Jesus and the Pharisees in

St Matthew's Gospel were fictions written after the fall of Jerusalem in response to the conditions of that time.

Nowadays it is not in Rome or in Canterbury that one finds the early chapters of Genesis taken literally, but in the fundamentalist evangelical churches that have proliferated, especially in the United States. In such communities it is common to speak with disdain of 'the enlightenment project'. But within traditional, mainstream Christian communities, the Enlightenment can fairly claim to have made many of its points.

19

The ethical legacy

One of the Enlightenment's major aims was to divorce morality from theology: to show that ethics did not need a basis in revelation and that a society could be cohesive without sharing a religion. Of all the Enlightenment's projects, this is the one that has had a continuous history over time and that has scored the most widespread success. The most elaborate attempt to construct an ethical system on a purely secular basis was the utilitarianism developed by Jeremy Bentham, as described in Chapter 14.

Bentham himself did not bring out what is the really significant difference between his utilitarianism and other moral systems. Hitherto most philosophers, because they believed in a natural law or natural rights, believed that there were some kinds of action that were intrinsically wrong, and should never be done, irrespective of any consideration of the consequences. But Bentham insisted that the morality of actions should be judged by their foreseen consequences, and that there is no category of act that may not, in special circumstances, be justified by its effects. He rejected the notion of natural law on the grounds that no two people could agree what it was. He was scornful of natural rights, believing that real rights could only be conferred by positive law; and his greatest scorn was directed to the idea that natural rights could not be overridden: 'Natural rights is simple nonsense: natural and imprescriptible rights, rhetorical nonsense – nonsense upon stilts' (*B* 2, 501). If there is no natural law and there are no natural rights, then no class of actions can be ruled out in advance of the consideration of the consequences of such an action in a particular case.

'The greatest happiness of the greatest number' is an impressive slogan; but when probed it turns out to be riddled with ambiguity. We may ask 'Greatest number of *what*?' Should we add 'voters' or 'citizens' or 'males' or 'human beings' or 'sentient beings'? It makes a huge difference which answer we give. Throughout the two centuries of utilitarianism's history, most of its devotees would probably give the answer 'human beings', and this is most likely the answer Bentham would have given. He did not advocate women's suffrage, but only because he thought that to do so would provoke outrage; in principle he thought that on the basis of the greatest happiness principle, 'the claim of [the female] sex is, if not still better, at least altogether as good as that of the other' (*B* ix, 108–9).

In recent years many utilitarians have extended the happiness principle beyond humankind to other sentient beings, claiming that animals have equal claims with human beings. Bentham himself did not go as far as this, and he would have rejected the idea that animals have rights. But by making the supreme moral criterion a matter of sensation he made it appropriate to consider animals as belonging to the same moral community as ourselves, since animals as well as humans feel pleasure and pain. This, in the long term, proved to be one of the most significant consequences of Bentham's break with the classical and Christian moral tradition, which placed supreme moral value in activities not of the senses but of the reason, and regarded non-rational animals as standing outside the moral community.

A second question about the principle of utility is this: when we are measuring the happiness of a population, do we consider only total happiness or should we also consider average happiness? Should we take account of the distribution of happiness as well as of its quantity? If so, then we have to strike a difficult balance between quantity of happiness and quantity of people.

This and similar problems exercised Bentham's successors in the utilitarian tradition, the most distinguished of whom was John Stuart Mill. Mill restated the grand principle as follows:

> The ultimate end, with reference to and for the sake of which all other things are desirable (whether we are considering our own good or that of other people), is an existence exempt as far as possible from pain, and as rich as possible in enjoyments, both in point of quantity and quality; the test of quality, and the rule for measuring it against quantity, being the preference felt by those who in their opportunities of experience, to which must be added their habits of self-consciousness and self-observation, are best furnished with the means of comparison.   (*U* 262)

Objections to utilitarianism come in two different forms. As a moral code it may be thought to be too strict, or too lax. Those who complain that it is too strict say that to insist that in every single action one should take account not just of one's own but of universal happiness is to demand a degree of altruism beyond the range of all but saints. Those who regard utilitarianism as too lax say that its abolition of absolute prohibitions on kinds of action opens a door for moral agents to persuade themselves that they are in the special circumstances that would justify an otherwise outrageous act.

In *Utilitarianism*, Mill offers a defence on both fronts. Against the allegation of excessive rigour he urges us to distinguish between a moral standard and a motive of action: utilitarianism, while offering universal happiness as the ultimate moral standard, does not require it to be the aim of every action. To those who allege laxity, he responds only with a *tu quoque*: all moral systems have to make room for conflicting obligations, and utility is not the only creed 'which is able to furnish us with excuses for evil doing, and means of cheating our own conscience' (*U* 277).

Utilitarianism, as invented by Bentham and modified by Mill, became and has remained the dominant moral tradition in Western liberal democracies. It is widely accepted even by religious writers in discussion with their secular counterparts. Few theologians nowadays present morality as a system of divine commands: things are right or wrong in themselves, and moral judgements are our own responsibility. If we obey God we do so because we see in him supreme goodness, and we must always be in a position to judge whether what is proposed in God's name is holy or wicked.

Such, for instance, is the view of Bishop Richard Harries in his *The Re-enchantment of Morality*, published by SPCK in 2008. It is possible, Harries maintains, to make valid ethical judgements without religious belief. What Christianity does is to add an extra dimension, an 'enchantment' to the moral life, by presenting it as a response to a gracious God as revealed in the person and teaching of Jesus. That teaching did not consist of commands, and Jesus was not, we are told, 'a literalist or a legislator'.

Armed with this template for the interpretation of the gospel, Harries explores Jesus' teaching in relation to four drivers of human behaviour: sex, money, power and fame. On these topics Harries' conclusions are always sensible and humane. But a secular reader is continually tempted to ask to what extent they are Christian. On divorce and homo-sexuality, for instance, his recommendations run counter to apparently plain texts of the Bible and to many centuries of teaching by all the churches. He would reply that individual items of Scripture and tradition are trumped by the overarching gospel imperative to love our neighbour. But the call to charity was no less known to Christian teachers of earlier ages than to moral theologians of the present century. One cannot help feeling that the developments of liberal thought in Christian churches are due not so much to deeper reflection on the Bible as to the teaching of secular moralists and the legacy of the Enlightenment.

20

The political legacy

Early enlightenment thinkers had no quarrel with the existence of monarchy – not even with absolute monarchy,
provided the monarch was enlightened. By the end of the
Enlightenment, however, the abolition of hereditary monarchy became one of the movement's major aims. In the
world of today that goal has been very largely achieved. To
be sure, quite a number of states are headed by hereditary
monarchs, some of them doing a very good job – but the
job is largely ceremonial and few such monarchs actually
rule. Very few states are governed by hereditary rulers, and
those that are stand out as outliers, whether in the Middle
East, in Africa or in North Korea. In the United States,
recent attempts to corral the presidency within a single
family, whether Republican or Democrat, have received a
chastening setback.

A constant aim of the Enlightenment, early or late, was to
constrain the arbitrary use of power by rulers of whatever
constitutional complexion. Most of the Enlightenment's
detailed aims in this area were codified in the United
Nations Universal Declaration of Human Rights, adopted
by the General Assembly on 10 December 1948. Beginning
with the statement that all human beings are born free and
equal in dignity and rights, the code includes a number
of articles that specify enlightenment concerns and echo
enlightenment language. For instance:

Article 3: Everyone has the right to life, liberty and security of person.
Article 5: No one shall be subjected to torture or to cruel, inhuman or degrading treatment or punishment.
Article 9: No one shall be subjected to arbitrary arrest, detention or exile.

The fourth article of the Declaration states that no one shall be held in slavery or servitude: slavery and the slave trade shall be prohibited in all their forms. It would not be correct to regard this as a further triumph of enlightenment values. With honourable exceptions, such as Priestley and his associates, prominent thinkers of the movement seem to have had a blind spot where slavery was concerned. There is no entry on the topic in Voltaire's *Philosophical Dictionary*, and both Franklin and Jefferson kept slaves. Notoriously the United States, the Enlightenment's most splendid political creation, did not remove the scourge of slavery until four score and seven years after its foundation. It was in fact evangelical Christians who led the campaigns against the slave trade. It was not David Hume but his great foe Samuel Johnson who raised a toast in Oxford: 'Here's to the next insurrection of the Negroes in the West Indies.'

The right of freedom of expression, stated in Article 19, is said to include the right to receive and impart information and ideas through any media. This corresponds to the enlightenment concern – echoed in an amendment of the US Constitution – with the freedom of the press. Article 20 takes the freedom of expression a stage further by proclaiming the right of peaceful assembly and association.

The Declaration is not a legally binding document, and it would be absurd to claim that its articles have been universally observed in the period since its publication. Though some of its provisions have had significant legal effect in individual countries, it remains an aspiration rather than a code of laws. There are several subsequent resolutions of the UN General Assembly that reflect enlightenment values: for instance, the 1960 declaration on the granting of independence to colonial countries and peoples. This declaration has been very largely put into effect: some states may remain colonies *de facto*, but no longer *de jure*. However, this does not means that Article 15 of the original declaration, conferring on everyone the right to a nationality, has been fully implemented: there are still millions of stateless people. Sadly, again, it cannot be claimed as a universal truth that within ex-colonial states other human rights are now better maintained than they were under imperial rule.

Torture, and in particular judicial torture, was a major concern of several of the leading enlightenment thinkers, and it has been the topic of several UN resolutions, notably the 1975 declaration on protection from torture and the 1984 convention against torture and other cruel, inhuman or degrading treatment or punishment. The convention defines torture as the deliberate official infliction of severe pain or suffering to obtain information or a confession, or as punishment for an act alleged, or for purposes of intimidation or coercion. Every nation is obliged to prevent acts of torture, and the convention states that no exceptional circumstances whatever, whether a state of war, internal political instability or any other public emergency, may be invoked as a justification for torture.

Since the convention came into force in 1987 the majority of states have become party to the convention, and a parallel convention was adopted in Europe in the same year. The provisions of these conventions have had significant effect in several jurisdictions, including the United Kingdom during the troubles in Northern Ireland. Sadly, however, torture has continued to be employed by the governments of states that in other respects are among the most enlightened, and there can be no guarantee that its use will diminish in future.

The European Convention on Human Rights, originally signed in Rome in 1950 and since then ratified by most European countries, whether or not members of the European Union, echoes the UN declaration. However, it goes into greater detail on the cases in which individuals can be deprived of their liberty and the circumstances into which emergency derogation from the convention is justified. It also makes clear that the right to freedom of expression does not prevent states from requiring the licensing of cinema and broadcasting. To oversee this convention there is a European Court of Human Rights. This is not an appeal court with power to overturn decisions of national tribunals, rather a review body that has a duty to bring to the attention of individual governments any case where their actions contravene the rights specified in the convention. In several cases decisions of the court have led to improvements in local legislation.

The UN Declaration was issued in the year that marked the second centenary of the publication of Montesquieu's *Spirit of the Laws*. In 2015 we marked the second centenary of the Battle of Waterloo, which led to the return of the pre-Enlightenment international order. We may recall that the very notion of human rights was itself an enlightenment invention. At the present time, the two international bodies that have most clearly articulated the scope of human rights, the United Nations and the European Court, are the subject of influential criticism on both sides of the Atlantic. We must hope that the twentieth-century Enlightenment does not come to as abrupt an end in the twenty-first century as its eighteenth-century predecessor did in the nineteenth.

Glossary

agnosticism   belief that nothing is known about the existence or non-existence of God

atheism   belief that there is no God

deism   belief in God as creator, coupled with rejection of revelation

dissenter   English member of Christian denomination other than Church of England

empiricism   belief that the senses (sight, etc.) are the only true sources of knowledge

Jansenist   member of austere Roman Catholic group pessimistic in theology

Jesuit   member of male religious order founded by St Ignatius of Loyola

original sin   state of sinfulness believed to be inherited from Adam in conception

predestination   God's choice of individuals to be saved, made before they exist

prelapsarian   prior to the fall of Adam

sacrament   solemn religious rite in Christian churches

scepticism   belief that nothing can be known with certainty

theism   belief in the existence of God

theodicy   defence of the justice of God's activity in the world

Tory   member of British political party that preceded the Conservatives

Whig   member of British political party that preceded the Liberals

Further reading

Berlin, Isaiah, *Against the Current: Essays in the History of Ideas* (London: Hogarth Press, 1979).

Besterman, Theodore, *Voltaire* (Oxford: Blackwell, 1969).

Broadie, Alexander, *A History of Scottish Philosophy* (Edinburgh: Edinburgh University Press, 2009).

Cronk, Nicholas, *The Cambridge Companion to Voltaire* (Cambridge: Cambridge University Press, 2009).

Gray, John, *Enlightenment's Wake: Politics and Culture at the Close of the Modern Age* (London and New York: Routledge, 2007).

Haakonssen, Knud, *The Cambridge Companion to Adam Smith* (Cambridge: Cambridge University Press, 2006).

Haakonssen, Knud, *The Cambridge History of Eighteenth-Century Philosophy* (Cambridge: Cambridge University Press, 2006).

Himmelfarb, Gertrude, *The Roads to Modernity: The British, French, and American Enlightenments* (London: Vintage Books, 2008).

Hunter, M. and Wootton, D., *Atheism from the Reformation to the Enlightenment* (Oxford: Clarendon Press, 1992).

Israel, Jonathan, *Democratic Enlightenment, Philosophy, Revolution and Human Rights, 1750–1790* (Oxford: Oxford University Press, 2011).

Lloyd, Genevieve, *Enlightenment Shadows* (Oxford: Oxford University Press, 2013).

Mossner, E. C., *The Life of David Hume* (Oxford: Clarendon Press, 1970).

Norman, Jesse, *Edmund Burke* (London: Collins, 2013).

Porter, Roy, *Enlightenment: Britain and the Creation of the Modern World* (London: Allen Lane, 2000).

Further reading

Reed, T. J., *Light in Germany* (Chicago and London: University of Chicago Press, 2015).

Robertson, John, *The Enlightenment: A Very Short Introduction* (Oxford: Oxford University Press, 2015).

Taylor, Charles, *A Secular Age* (Cambridge, MA: Harvard University Press, 2008).

Trevor-Roper, Hugh, *History and the Enlightenment* (New Haven, CT and London: Yale University Press, 2010).

Yolton, John W. et al. *The Blackwell Companion to the Enlightenment* (Oxford: Blackwell, 1991).

Index

Note: The locators in **bold** indicate a definition of the term as found in the Glossary.

Index

Index

Index